SOARING
AS EAGLES

SOARING
AS EAGLES

Stop Struggling Start Soaring

Leif Hetland

In my 54 years of ministry I have never known or esteemed anyone higher in the Kingdom work than I do the young evangelist, Leif Hetland. This wonderful Norwegian-American has confirmed his love for God, his commitment to the gospel, and his obedience to follow the Holy Spirit, in incredible submission.

Charles Carrin
Charles Carrin Ministries

Serving with Leif Hetland has been a wonderful blessing for me. His commitment to God and His people has truly been an inspiration in my life. Our Father's love has transformed Leif and he continues to carry that same healing love to the ends of the earth.

Lenny LeBlanc
Songwriter and Worship Leader

I strongly recommend the book *Soaring As Eagles* by Leif Hetland. As Leif's pastor, I have watched him live out the truths in this book. He makes powerful spiritual applications of the natural truths about the Eagle so that believers can soar. You will be encouraged to explore the heights of intimacy with God as you journey through these informative and inspirational pages.

Eddie Lawrence, D.Min.
Senior Pastor of Faith Church
Author of *Breath of God*, Nelson Books

I know of no greater anointing resting on anyone greater than that which is upon Leif. He continues with every trip to that section of the world to experience amazing results. We all know that a part of the sowing and reaping principle has to do with the quality of the soil. I know of no greater, richer, or fertile soil than this ministry.

Jack Taylor
Dimensions Ministries

I regard Leif Hetland as a most unusual servant of Jesus Christ. My wife and I believe in him, support him, and recommend him and his ministry far and wide. I believe in him with all my heart. Few, it seems to me, have the combination of his courage and open doors.

Dr. R. T. Kendall
RT Kendall Ministries

It is an honor to recommend the ministry of my friend, Leif Hetland. With simple words, He reveals the message of profound love that can be received and understood by any heart. His depth of commitment, humble spirit and child-like faith always makes me feel I am in the presence of one of the "great ones".

Karen Wheaton
Musical Artist

The first time I met him I was so impressed with the love of God that flows from his heart and the passion that he has for the lost world. I believe the Holy Spirit has given Leif the Father's heart. I have known only a few men who exemplify the depth of God's love and passion as does Leif.

E. M. Shell
Pastor of Christ Chapel, Florence, AL

Leif has a dynamic anointing, a strong evangelistic gift, and a healing ministry which includes an incredible revelatory teaching on the Father's love. Because of his great exploits in ministry to the un-reached people groups of the world, his life reads like an action thriller novel. He's the real deal! Every time I see him, I am challenged to go deeper with God.

Gary Oates
Gary Oates Ministries
Author of *Open My Eyes, Lord*

Leif Hetland is a contagious reflection of the Father's heart. More than talking about what he knows, he ministers from who he is. Our lives have been powerfully impacted by his life. His revelation of the Father's love is foundational truth that sets hearts free from lies and hindrances. We are grateful that the Lord is sending gifts like Leif to His Body!

Dave Hess
Senior Pastor of Christ Community Church, Camp Hill, PA

I have been privileged to minister alongside Leif in larger Christian conferences and in smaller meetings with several Christian psychiatrists from around the world. Whether ministering in the United States or on his trips to the nations, it is awesome to see the Lord's anointing on Leif and Jennifer. I have myself received an amazing impartation of the Father's love from Leif, and my own professional work and ministry of inner healing has never been the same since that day.

Stephen Mory, M.D.
Past President, Psychiatric Section, Christian Medical Association

CONTENTS

Foreword

God hides things for us and not from us. Leif Hetland has successfully discovered the process of growth and promotion that God hid in the life of the eagle. I have had the privilege of hearing Leif minister these truths in person, and have looked forward to having this treasure in print. This remarkable story is not theory. It is a record of the painful triumph of this yielded individual to the purposes of God. I heartily recommend this book in the same way I have enthusiastically recommended the messenger. You will be challenged and changed as you enter your season of promotion.

Bill Johnson
Author of *When Heaven Invades Earth*

Foreword

Leif Hetland is one of my heroes of the faith who risks his life holding healing events among the Pakistanis, the communists, and in war torn areas of Africa, including the large refugee camps. God has truly anointed him and uses him mightily. When former missionaries heard about what Leif was doing they found it difficult to believe the stories about the crowds he was drawing, and how openly he preached about Jesus. But, when they saw the videos and heard the Urdu language being spoken, they saw that it was true.

Soaring As Eagles is Leif's newest book which explains some of the revelation God gave to Leif regarding the similarity between the Lord's process of restoration and the molting process that an eagle goes through. Many of the insights Leif shares at his Soaring As Eagles Conferences are revealed throughout this book. These insights from the revelation God gave Leif will encourage anyone who is going through a difficult time in their life and will give them a better perspective to understand what God is doing in this difficult period in their lives. It will also encourage anyone who feels like there is more than what they are presently experiencing. You will learn how to soar as an eagle.

Just as I highly recommend Leif's ministry to pastor's, I highly recommend this book to everyone. Read and learn how to understand and adjust yourself to what may be God's plan for your life. If you learn the lesson you will come out even more anointed of the Lord and more compassionate than before.

Randy Clark
Author of *There Is More!*

Acknowledgments

I want to acknowledge the best wife a man could ever hope for, Jennifer. How I honor and admire her as a person, as an Eagle Christian, as a mother to four eaglets, and as a partner in the harvest.

Jennifer and I want to thank our secretary and personal assistant, Jana Jordan, who makes us look better than we truly are.

Thank you Ryan Adair for endless hours of research, typing, editing, and giving your best.

Thanks to Dr. Eddie Lawrence, our pastor and friend. Eddie, I owe so much to you. Thank you with all of my heart.

If there is success in my life it is because of a lot of people.

Thanks Jack and Freide Taylor, Charles Carrin, R.T. Kendall, Ron Phillips, Eddie McClain, Mark Jordan, Kent Martin, Paul Corfman, Carl Robertson, and Bjornar Heimstad. I love you.

Thanks to Randy Clark and Bill Johnson for the foreword and for their friendship.

Thank you, Lord, for all these wonderful Fathers, friends, and family who have enriched my life in so many ways.

Introduction

OVER THE PAST YEAR, THE FATHER HAS BEEN TEACHING ME about being what I call an *eagle believer*. Through various experiences with the Lord, and reading many books about the subject, God has been illuminating for me and teaching me about how a believer's walk with the Lord is similar to that of an eagle. Every time the Lord revealed for me a certain characteristic or aspect of an eagle, He was inviting me into a deeper revelation of Him, and myself as His son. The spiritual implications were astonishing upon my life. The more I discovered, the more I wanted to learn about this wonderful and majestic bird. The Holy Spirit used the eagle to show me who I truly am, my relationship to others, and most importantly, my relationship to the Father. It is out of this revelation this book was born.

After a wonderful season of soaring with the eagles – preaching at many conferences, traveling two-thirds of the year, and turning down more invitations than I could accept – I was grounded. All of the sudden, it all stopped and came to an end. Like an eagle, it was then that I began a season of molting in my own life and ministry. Suddenly, I wasn't preaching as much as I used to, or traveling as much. I was still receiving invitations, but I felt like it was a time to take off from *doing* what I had been doing, and begin to *be* with the Lord once again. It was now a time to begin waiting on the Lord.

Don't get me wrong. I spent time with the Lord while I was doing all of these things – I had to; my life depended on it. But I became so busy in my life and ministry that it was distracting me from focusing completely on Him. I was too busy to be able to hear His intimate voice speak so clearly to me in ways I needed as a son.

By this time in my ministry, I hadn't given much thought to eagles, or any bird for that matter. I knew what an eagle was and I understood some of the symbolism they carried throughout the Bible, but I was about to enter a school that was taught by the Holy Spirit. He would begin to teach me about the spiritual significance of an eagle and how it relates to a believer's life and ministry. Furthermore, God also likens Himself to an eagle in a number of Biblical passages.

Why the eagle? Why not another bird? Why did God use this majestic bird and not another throughout the Bible to reveal so much to His people? As we open the Word and allow it to speak to us, the Holy Spirit will provide the answer to our questions. I'm praying that what the Lord reveals to your heart through this book will lead you into greater transformation – greater godliness and Christlikeness.

Let me warn you – this process will take you to the point of death and many will die because of it. I am not speaking of physical death, of course. But God will cause a death to come to you where it is no longer you who are living, but Christ is living

His life through you (see Galatians 2:20-21). Are you excited now? You will be!

One of the purposes of this book will help you to build your life upon Christ, the Solid Rock. You will form a solid foundation from which you will learn to soar like eagles. This is a wonderful opportunity to get your spiritual feathers, learn how to tend them, clean them, and pluck them out when necessary, and to even help other eagles. Most of all, however, it will be a time where you learn to SOAR in the high places with God! You will soar into the realm of the impossible – the realm of the supernatural.

> I have been crucified with Christ; it is no longer I who live, but Christ lives in me; and the life which I now live in the flesh I live by faith in the Son of God, who loved me and gave Himself for me. I do not set aside the grace of God; for if righteousness comes through the law, then Christ died in vain.
>
> Galatians 2:20-21

Are you tired of flapping your wings? Are you feverishly going about God's work but feeling increasingly frustrated and dissatisfied? Do you hear sermons telling you that "His burden is light" and you want to scream "Oh yeah? Not Mine!" Do you ever read the words of Jesus saying, "My yoke is easy and My burden is light" (see Matthew 11:28-30), and wonder why you don't seem to be experiencing it. I believe that as you read this book you will be refreshed. You will learn to become sensitive to the currents of the wind and learn to soar on eagles' wings.

Before I go on, I must say that I'm very indebted to the writings and teachings of men and women like Col Stringer, Joyce Meyer, and Perry Stone for research on this subject. They have influenced me greatly in my pursuit of an understanding of the eagle as it relates to God and to believers.

Let us now go on to define and explain what I mean by the term *eagle believer* and see how God wants to teach us from the things that He has created. You are created to soar!

CHAPTER ONE

Eagle Believers

Defining An Eagle Believer

I BELIEVE THIS REVELATION OF *EAGLE BELIEVERS* IS NOT ONLY for me, but also for the Body of Christ as a whole. Not only is He calling me to rise up to this position with Him; He is calling the entire Church to learn how to soar on wings like eagles. Beloved, the Father is calling you and me to be *eagle believers*. What do I mean by the term *eagle believer*? Let me explain a little bit.

Throughout the entire Bible, Old Testament to New, the believer's walk with the Lord is likened to that of an eagle. We are going to see through this book and the books to follow, how our lives as Christians relate to that of an eagle and how we can learn from its ways of life. The eagle is used in Scripture as an example of Christian life and carries very important spiritual implications made to impact our life in a powerful way. To put it simply: an *eagle believer* is someone who learns to wait upon the Lord in intimacy so they will gain fresh strength to soar through the storms of life.

Did you know that over thirty-two times the Bible uses eagles as an example to help us as believers learn from? Why is that? It is because eagles are unusual birds that are born to soar higher and fly faster than any other bird in creation. As God's *eagle believers*, we are raised up and made to soar in heavenly realms with Christ Jesus (see Ephesians 2:4-6).

Many people might believe at this point that somehow we're putting undue attention and worship on the "creature rather than the Creator" (Romans 1:25). I don't want you to think that as you read this book. I serve God more than anything in this world and in no way am I worshipping the creation of eagles. However, I have come to understand that God has much to teach us through what He has created. Let us look at some passages of Scripture about how God longs to teach us through His creation.

> But God, who is rich in mercy, because of His great love with which He loved us, even when we were dead in trespasses, made us alive together with Christ (by grace you have been saved), and raised us up together, and made us sit together in the heavenly places in Christ Jesus.
>
> Ephesians 2:4-6

Teaching Through Creation

The story of creation is covered in the first two chapters of the Bible, specifically in Genesis chapters one and two. In those two chapters, God creates everything we see around us. Everything of God's creation was created in those six days and when He finished, He decided to take a rest on the seventh day. He said after each day of creation that everything He created was "good" (see Genesis 1:4, 10, 12, 18, 21, 25, 31). He must have been pleased with how the creation was beginning to take shape.

The first three days God created the light, sea, skies, the earth, and the vegetation. On the next three days, He created objects to fill what He created on the three previous days – the sun, moon, stars, birds, fish, animals and eventually human beings. The first three days there was form, and then the second three days there was fullness. It is God's ultimate purpose to fill the form with fullness.

On the fourth day of creation, God created the sun, moon, stars and the luminaries to carry the light He created on the first day. Do you understand that light was created before the sun, moon, or stars? God created light before He created the objects to hold the light. On the fifth day, He created birds and fish to fill the skies and seas He created on the second day. Then, on the sixth day, He created man and animals to fill and consume the earth and vegetation that He created on the third day. You see, God made the form, then came the fullness to fill the form.

If God goes through all of this work of creation, then I believe He wants to speak to us through everything He created. His voice can be heard through His creation without actually worshipping the creation itself. Creation is not something that we worship, but it is a means through which we are able to hear the voice of our Father. Again, is must be said here that it is not the only means of hearing His voice, nor is it the primary means by which we hear His voice. It is only one way out of many that we are able to hear the voice of God.

Many of the Biblical authors agree with, and understood the concept that God wants to speak to His people from and through His creation. Job seems to believe that God can and does speak to people through what He has created.

Job's friends seem to have spoke to him, what they thought, were the words and wisdom of God. However, Job responded by telling them they were acting as false witness's on behalf of God. Though Job may doubt some of God's justice, he doesn't seem to be doubting that God will punish them for their false words. They would do better to listen to what He has to say or to God's creation than what they are so vainly speaking. He says,

> But now ask the beasts, and they will teach you;
> And the birds of the air, and they will tell you;
> Or speak to the earth, and it will teach you;
> And the fish of the sea will explain to you.
> Who among all these does not know
> That the hand of the LORD has done this,
> In whose hand is the life of every living thing,
> And the breath of all mankind?
> Does not the ear test words
> And the mouth taste its food?
> Wisdom is with aged men,

And with length of days, understanding.

(Job 12:7-12)

Job understood that God was able to speak through what He has created. He believed God's voice could be speaking to His people through the birds of the air and the beasts of the earth. Job says when we look to the beasts and the birds of the air they will "teach" and "tell" us things about God. How much more could be benefit in our pursuit of God if we understood this? We could learn to hear from God throughout our whole day, rather than just in our quiet time in the morning.

Furthermore, David points out the heavens, and *all* that is within them, declare the glory of God. This, in my opinion, would obviously include anything that inhabits the heavens, whether it is the sun or some type of bird. It seems as though the heaven, and all that is contained therein, declares the glory and voice of God in some way or another. David says,

The heavens declare the glory of God;

And the firmament shows His handiwork.

Day unto day utters speech,

And night unto night reveals knowledge.

There is no speech nor language

Where their voice is not heard.

(Psalm 19:1-3)

When David says the heavens "declare the glory of God," he is saying that the heavens are "inscribing the glory of God" so that others can see and read about it. David understood that God wanted to speak through creation as well as wanting others to hear from what has been created.

Paul also teaches us a lesson about God's voice being heard through His creation. He is revealing a principle of God that can, without doubt, be carried over into God's voice being heard through creation. God will often reveal truth through creation and natural means, and what He has created will have a deeper meaning – a symbolic, spiritual meaning for us to draw from. The apostle says this,

> However, the spiritual is not first, but the natural,
> and afterward the spiritual. (1 Corinthians 15:46)

Many times God will speak to us through natural means; but His ultimate purpose is to reveal some sort of spiritual truth to our hearts. Friends, if these Biblical writers believed in the voice of God through creation, then how much more should we?

God is speaking a language to us by the things He has created. Paul, in the book of Romans says that everyone has some understanding of God even if they have not heard the Word of God being preached to them. He says that God's attributes are "clearly seen, being understood by the things that are made, even His eternal power and Godhead, so that they are without excuse..." (see Romans 1:18-21). No one will have an excuse when they stand before the throne of God because they didn't know about Him. When we see all that was created, we know that Someone must have created it. That Someone could only be God.

Creation Is Speaking

It is easy to see from the Biblical authors that they believed in God's voice being heard through what has been created. It is theme that runs throughout the entire Bible. Creation reveals God's voice to such a degree that if you have never heard the Gospel preached, then you will be judged according to what has been created. If the Biblical authors agree with God's voice being heard through creation, then maybe we should take heed. God wants to speak to us through what has been created – we must learn to listen.

The part of creation God has been speaking to me about is that of the bird kingdom. Namely, I've been studying what God has to say about eagles. Throughout this book, and other books to follow, I want to take you on a journey through what the Lord has been teaching me about this bird and how it relates to our lives. I want to share with you what the Lord has been teaching me about being an *eagle believer*.

CHAPTER TWO

You Are Created To Soar

I WANT TO SHARE A STORY THAT WILL ILLUSTRATE THE PURPOSE behind this book. It is a story of fulfilling one's potential. It is a story of rising above the status quo of religion and tradition and doing something that seems that no one else is doing. It is a story of walking in the supernatural in the midst of a natural and common world. In fact, it is a story of each of us and what we are created to do in God. We are created for so much more than what we know. Are we going to fulfill it in our lifetime? The story goes like this.

On a mountain peak far above a farm, a farmer had taken an egg from the nest of an eagle. He had placed it under a sitting hen that hatched it with a brood of little chickens. With much patience, he had raised it and tried to tame it and make it a domestic bird just like the chickens it was continually surrounded by.

From the very beginning, the eagle had not fit in to the routine of the chickens. It walked alone finding no fellowship with the other chicks or the hen. It looked different, talked different, and wasn't particular to the food of the chickens; in fact, the eagle just seemed to be out of place. Even though from the day it was hatched, the eagle had known no environment but the domestic life around it. But from deep within, something of the wild free nature of the eagle cried out that this was not its home. Some-thing kept telling him that he was destined for so much more.

As it grew larger, its wings were clipped just like the rest of the chickens. Unable to fly, it sat in the barnyard daily looking upward. Its body was confined to the earth, but its heart knew it was called to greater heights and heavenly places above. For some time, the farmer had failed to clip its wings with the rest of the chickens. The young eagle knew this and stretched its wings out to feel the wind go beneath them. As it did this, it caught sight of another eagle soaring on the wind high above the storm clouds. At that moment, the ears of the eagle caught the sound of a sharp, pierc-ing cry from the eagle that was soaring so high in the sky. Sud-denly, as the wind caught beneath its wings and lifted it from the ground, it let out a shrill scream of victory and freedom, leaving the barnyard forever and soaring into the sky to meet those of its own kind.

> The eagle that soars in the upper air does not worry about crossing rivers.

Some of you can understand the purpose of this story with-out me even explaining it. Many believers have an eagle within them who is waiting to fly. So many have settled among the chickens in the chicken pen and never experienced the joy of rising up, mounting up to higher places, and getting high enough to be able to enjoy life with God and to be able to look at life from God's eyes and perspective.

Some of you have eaten the same food as the chickens, got your wings clipped, stayed inside a caged pen, while recognizing a deep cry in your spirit for more of God. God is raising up *eagle saints* who are willing to go through the process of molting so that the new feathers can grow and they can leave the chicken yard to mount up like eagles and to run without growing weary and to walk without fainting.

Many of us know the Scripture in Isaiah 40:31 all too familiarly. We quote it, talk about it, and even preach about it without knowing the fullness of what it contains. Over the past year, it has been the main Scripture that has influenced my life in so many different ways. When I ask questions and wonder why I'm going through all of these storms in my personal life, I return to this Scripture. Again and again, I've gained fresh insight and daily strength from meditating upon it.

I believe in these days, when God is calling the church to be *eagle believers*, He wants to bring wisdom and revelation about this passage that we have never known before. God is inviting you and me to be an *eagle believer* today. With every revelation that God gives, He will also open up a door to invite us in to experience what He has just revealed.

Let us look at what Isaiah says to those going through the storms of life,

> But those who wait on the LORD shall renew
> their strength,

They shall mount up with wings like eagles,

They shall run and not be weary,

They shall walk and not faint.

(40:31)

This is a tremendous passage and we repeatedly see the Word of God illustrating for us what it is to be like an eagle. We are going to take a journey throughout the Bible to see the importance of the eagle to the Biblical writers and how this majestic bird can teach us so many powerful truths. However, right now we are going to look at some of the characteristics of the eagle that we know from natural science so we can begin to draw some spiritual implications from it.

CHAPTER THREE

Characteristics Of The Eagle

THERE ARE MANY DIFFERENT SPECIES OF EAGLES THROUGHOUT the world today. Probably one of the most famous species of eagle in North America is the North American Bald Eagle. It is defined, not for its baldness as the name describes, but because its head is white and the rest of its body is dark brown in color. This gives it a look of baldness. The Bald Eagle is also renowned because of its incredible comeback in the face of extinction. However, when the Bible speaks of an eagle, it is usually referring to a Golden Eagle or Imperial Eagle, not the Bald Eagle. Nevertheless, we believe God wants to speak to us from *all* of His creation. We are going to look at some facts of the eagle species in general and listen to what God has to say.

Name

The actual Hebrew word for "eagle," as found in the Bible, is the word *neser.* Two root meanings have been suggested for *neser.* The first suggestion is "gleaming flash" or "thrusting sound" (G.R. Driver), obviously noted for its speed and swiftness. The second meaning suggested for the Hebrew word *ne-*

ser is to "tear with the beak" or "to lacerate" (H.B. Tristram). This second definition is because of the way an eagle will tear apart its prey after they have caught it.

I want us to define what an eagle is from the dictionary before we look at some of its characteristics. I want to do this because I believe that we can learn a lot by how the bird is defined. I'm sure all of us know what an eagle is and most of us even know what some species of eagles look like. However, I don't know how many of us would actually know what defines an eagle – what makes an eagle, an eagle.

> Eagles are known for their strength, size, keenness of vision, and their gracefulness in flight.

Merriam-Webster s Collegiate Dictionary defines an eagle as "any of various diurnal birds of the accipiter family noted for their strength, size, keenness of vision, and powers of flight." It is interesting that an eagle isn't defined by its color, its maturity, or even how far they can fly. An eagle is defined as any type of large predatory bird that comes from the hawk family, which can be found in all parts of the world. The hawk family would include kites, hawks, buzzards, and certain vultures, as well as eagles. Out of the entire Hawk Family, the only species that is confined to North America is the Bald Eagle. All the other types of eagles can be found in different places of the world.

Eagles are diurnal birds, meaning they are a bird that flies and is awake only during the daytime. An eagle will never be seen flying or hunting during the night. The other four attributes that define an eagle according to *Merriam-Webster s Dictionary* are their strength, size, keenness of vision, and powers or gracefulness of flight. Other dictionaries say they are also known for their sharp beak and talons, their incredible wingspan, their mating patterns, as well as the way they care for their young in nests. Throughout these series of books, we're going to examine every one of these aspects and relate it to the believer's life today. We can learn great things from this incredible bird and draw some amazing spiritual principles so our lives will be changed.

Size

Eagles are similar in size to the other birds in the Hawk Family, but are larger both in length and in wingspan. They are only about thirty to forty-five inches in length, depending upon the species of eagle. The wingspan of the eagle is more impressive than their length, being up to twice the size of the bird itself. Their wings have been measured at over eight feet in width, which is incredible for a bird! As you can see from this enormous wingspan, these birds were created by God to soar high in the heavens.

> The Bald Eagle is the second largest bird of prey in North America, after the California Condor.

Some species of eagles can weigh up to fifteen pounds. With most of the different types of species of eagles, the female will be larger than the male. Even though a female can weigh up to fifteen pounds, the males will only weigh between eight and ten pounds. The males always seem to be the smaller bird of the two. As you can see, this bird is incredible in its size and wing-span.

Life Span

An eagle has an long life span for any type of bird. Most of the species of eagles live up to forty or fifty years in the wild. Even though they can live up to that long in the wild, the average age for an eagle is about thirty-five years old.

Amazingly, research proves that eagles can live much longer in captivity than out of it. There have been specific instances of eagles that have been known to live up to be one hundred years old when in held in captivity.

Nesting Patterns

An eagle will build its nest high in a fork of a tree or on a ledge of a cliff. The cliff is definitely preferred over the tree, but the tree will often suffice if there is not a cliff around to build a nest in.

They build their nests of twigs and sticks and line it with fur, leaves, feathers, moss, and other soft materials to provide com-fort, and so they are able to rest, raise their offspring. Their nests are added to repeatedly, year after year, becoming enormous. Because they are continually added to, there have been some nests that have actually weighed over one thousand pounds!

Eagles usually live and build their homes near large bodies of water like lakes, rivers, marshes, and seacoasts where there are plenty of fish to eat and many trees and crags to nest in. They are territorial in their nesting and will do almost anything to keep other eagles out of their territory.

Mating Patterns

Not only are eagles interested in building enormous nests, they also have other attributes of a healthy home life. Namely, they have good marriages. Eagles are solitary birds that are said to mate for life. An eagle will only select another mate if its faithful mate should die – and this without wasting any time.

An eagle reaches sexual maturity at about four to five years of age. At this time, the energy of an eagle will begin to be focused on finding a mate and raising offspring. It is at this point in life where everything else becomes second place and they give their full attention to finding a mate.

An eagle has the ability to breed every year, though some choose not too. Nobody knows for sure, but some think that availability of food, nesting space, and weather all have something to do with their lack of mating.

Offspring

The female eagle will lay about two to three eggs per year, this usually occurring in the springtime. Only about fifty percent of the eaglets that hatch actually survive their first year of life due to various circumstances. It will take an eaglet about twelve weeks, or four months, to become full-grown and learn how to fly. However, the eaglets do not develop their markings until they are about three to four years of age. It is at this time where they will move away from their parental protection and seek their own mates and territories.

Parental Care

For the first part of the life of an eaglet, the male Golden Eagles will brood over newly hatched chicks, along with the female. But in most species of eagles, the male's role is to hunt for food, which he brings to the female at the nest; then she will give it to the young. The female will stay at or near the nest until the eaglets begin to develop their feathers. At this time, the male's role diminishes and the female begins to go out and hunt for the food and provide for the young. Once the male's role diminishes, the female takes completely over until the eaglet is old enough to make an effort for itself and able to survive on its own.

Feeding Patterns

Eagles are well equipped for hunting; their sharp talons and beaks, which can be as long as their heads, enable them to feed on fish. Eagles mostly eat fish during spawning season, whether they are dead or alive. Many times an eagle will swoop down and dip its feet into the lake or river to pluck fish up out of the water. An eagle can also carry off small animals up to half of its weight if that is what is chooses to eat.

An eagle will also feed on rodents and carrion, which is the rotting flesh of a dead animal, though this is not preferable. Their diet mainly consists of mammals, ranging in size from mice to deer. These would include ducks, muskrats, turtles, rabbits, snakes, and the like. Obviously, a deer is too much for them to pick up and carry off to eat, but there have been instances where a deer has been killed by an eagle. The eagle in this case would feed on the dead carcass right were it lies.

One very interesting fact of an eagle is that it is tremendously susceptible to toxins and poisons. This is because the toxins are able to go through each animal or plant that has been eaten throughout the food chain. By the time the eagle gets some prey, its prey has already eaten other prey, absorbing the toxins of the previous plant or animals that have been consumed. These toxins go right through the food chain until they all end up in the eagles system, since the eagle is at the top of the food chain. Toxins were one of the main reasons the Bald Eagle was almost extinct for a number of years.

Eyesight And Hearing

All eagles are known for their renowned eyesight. Eagles have two centers of focus in each eye, which means they are able to focus on an object in front of them at the same time as being able to focus on a different object on either side of them.

They have the ability to see fish in the water from hundreds of feet above while soaring, flying, or flapping their wings in flight. This is very special because most fish are counter-shaded, meaning they are darker on top than they are on the sides, making them very hard to see from above. I've been fishing before, and it is hard to spot fish from six feet above water, let alone hundreds of feet above water. Every once in a while a younger eagle will be seen making a mistake and attacking a plastic bottle or the like that is floating in the water because it thought it was some sort of fish from hundreds of feet above the water.

The eye of an eagle is almost the size of a humans, even though the bird itself is much smaller than a human. However, its sight is at least four times that of a human who has perfect vision. Eagles don't see in black in white like some other animals or birds do; they have color vision.

> An eagle has amazing eyesight for a bird. It is ruled mainly by what it can see and perceive. An eagle has an eye almost the size of a human, although it can see at least four times better than a human.

An eagle can identify a moving rabbit almost a mile away. If an eagle was flying at or sitting on a tree a thousand feet high, it could see prey moving in a three square mile radius of open country. An eagle's sight is the main way that it hunts – vision is its main sense that it is ruled by.

An eagle doesn't use its hearing as much as its eyesight. Because it is a bird that is mainly active during the day, it doesn't rely on its hearing as much as other birds do. That does not mean that an eagle has poor hearing; it can still locate other birds and animals with its hearing alone. However, because of its reliance on its keen eyesight, it doesn't need to rely on hearing as much as an owl or bat would. The reason a bird develops and is ruled by its hearing is because they hunt and fly mainly during the night. Not so with eagles – they are daytime birds only.

Flying Patterns

Eagles are not like other birds in the fact that they are born to soar. In fact, they live to soar above the storms of life. They do not have to continually flap their wings trying to get from one place to the other like most other birds do. Eagles fly the best when they are relaxed and soaring on the air thermals they catch. The flapping of their wings is only preparatory to get them to the good air currents so they are able to soar higher and fly faster.

Eagles will run to a storm while most other birds will run away from a storm. An eagle was created to soar in storms. The eagle is amazing in the fact that it has an innate ability to sense the motion of the currents of the wind and can fully utilize the currents to its advantage. It will perch on a tree for hours waiting for the prefect storm to come. There is something in an eagle that knows it was created for so much more than other birds.

The Enemy Of The Eagle

The only natural predator of the eagle is the serpent. If left unattended, the eagle's eggs or the eaglets themselves could easily become the serpent's dinner. The eagle has the ability to kill any serpent that comes its way; but it must be attentive in its watch.

Even though the serpent is a predator to the eagle, the eagle has the ability and power to send the serpent to its death. It will

> The only enemy of an eagle is the serpent. Through being attentive, the eagle has the ability to send the serpent to its death.

grab the serpent with its powerful talons and soar to great heights. It will then drop the snake from the great heights so that it will be crushed on the rocks below. Even though a snake is the only reptile that threatens the eagle, the seems to be no fear in the eagle when it comes to fighting against the attacks of the snake.

Wisdom Of Eagles

Eagles are very wise birds. They stand tall and proud when you look at them. They are very careful to avoid danger and they rarely attack humans. If an eagle is returning to its nest and it senses danger nearby, the eagle will circle the area around its nest to make sure danger is not anywhere near before returning to its nest. Eagles are always on the lookout for anything in their territory or anything that is abnormal. They are continually watching and aware of their surroundings to make sure nothing is going to harm them.

Molting Process

A very unusual aspect of the eagle, that is not known too much about, is the molting process it will go through toward the end of its life. Scientists tell us that when an eagle gets older, it goes through what is called a molting process. This is probably one of the least researched and most misunderstood aspects of an eagle. Because this molting takes place in private, there have been very few studies done of an eagle actually going through the molting process.

However, the story the researchers give goes something like this. Over time, the beak and talons of an eagle become encrusted with calcium. Thus, they are not as sharp as they once were. Their feathers become weighed down with dirt and oil. When these things take place, it obviously hinders their ability to hunt effectively. With all of the dirt and oil on its feathers, an eagle will begin to "whistle" while it is diving on its prey. With a sound like this coming from a bird, it makes hunting ineffective because the prey can hear them coming and have more time to run and hide before they are snatched up.

When an eagle gets to this point in its life, it will descend from the heights above and go to a rock below. Through the molting process, the eagle begins to lose its feathers by plucking them out one by one. Not only will an eagle pluck out all of its feathers, it will actually break off its beak by smashing it on a rock. It will rub its talons on the rock to rub them down until they are nubbins. Its vision is even said to be impaired so they don't have as keen as eyesight as before. At this point, the eagle becomes weak, vulnerable, and defenseless. Many eagles die during this point in life because they cannot hunt for themselves and they can't protect themselves against predators.

During this time, many eagles become dependent on their companion eagles for sustenance and nourishment. If they can survive the shame and exposure that molting produces, then the stripping process will pave the way for the eagle to become greater and stronger than it was before.

It is during this time that a wonderful thing happens to those who survive. Their feathers, beak, and talons will begin to grow back with greater vigor than ever before. Their beak and talons will be as sharp as ever and they will once again take to the skies. They will have a revitalized youth and vitality to them that they hadn't possessed since they were younger.

The Death Of An Eagle

Finally, an eagle has an amazing ability to sense when it is going to die. When it senses this, an eagle will leave its nest and fly to a rock so that it can prepare to die. It will fasten its talons on the front of the rock, then look into the rising or setting sun, then just die. They are gone just like that. It is interesting that it is always on a rock looking into the sun when they die. How prophetic is that of us? We are to stand on the Rock and look into the eyes of the Son!

I'm sure that many of you have seen some spiritual implications just as you read through the characteristics of this bird. We've learned of its characteristics and defined the attributes that make it an eagle. Let us now turn our attention to the importance of the eagle throughout history. We are about to see how this magnificent bird has influenced the life of common people, nations, as well as all of society around us.

CHAPTER FOUR

History Of The Eagle

The Influence Of An Eagle

MAN HAS BEEN INSPIRED BY THE EAGLE PROBABLY MORE THAN any other creature in God's creation. We have a fascination with this bird. It demands our respect like no other animal in the animal kingdom. The only other animal that seems to be closest to it in respect would be the lion, which seems to be considered the king of the ground.

The eagle stirs our adrenaline and captivates our attention like no other bird in the world. We are not amazed when we see a sparrow, an owl, a canary, or even a crow for that matter. Most of us wouldn't even take a second look at such birds as these. Some of the above mentioned birds would be considered by many of us as pests. Farmers put "scarecrows" in their fields to keep the crows away from their crops because the crow is considered to be a nuisance.

However, when we see an eagle soaring in the sky, we seem to stop our life and pause for a moment to watch this amazing creature catching air thermals and soaring so effortlessly. The eagle seems to control the air. William Blake, who was a poet and into visual arts, once said, "When thou seest an eagle, thou seest a portion of genius; lift up thy head!"[i]

The Significance Of An Eagle

For centuries, the eagle has been imprinted on the heart and mind of man and demanded respect more than any other bird. We have used eagles to name places or mountains around us. They are found in such names as Eagle Corner, Bald Eagle, New Eagle, Black Eagle, Red Eagle, Gold Eagle, White Eagle, War Eagle, Eagleville, Eagleton, Eaglelet to identify villages, cities, bridges, mills, groves, stations, etc. There are also Eagle Lakes, Eagle Mountains, Eagle Rivers, Eagle Islands, and Eagle Forts without number. There are also television channels, newspapers and the like that bear the name of this bird.

> The eagle has influenced our culture and society more than any other bird in the world.

The eagle permeates everything around us in our culture and many cultures of the world. There can be no doubt that this bird has a major significance throughout history as well as a major affect upon us today.

We also use eagles to define certain truths in our speech. We say a person has *eagle wit* if we think that a person is very smart or has sharp humor. We say a person has an *eagle eye* if they have an incredible eye for detail or see something others cannot in the distance. We say a person is an *eagle pilot* if the

---

[i] This quote was accessed off http://www.brainyquote.com/quotes/quotes/w/williambla150115.html on June, 3 2006.

person is the best, top fighter pilot of their class. In the United States, they used to have a gold coin worth ten dollars called the *eagle*. The word eagle also caries over into sports. We use the word *eagle* and *double eagle* in golf to signify a person getting two or three strokes respectively under par.

For centuries, the eagle has been recognized by many nations as the king of birds. Eagles, impressive in both size and beauty, have long been symbols of royal power, authority, and even courage. They have appeared on coins, seals, flags, and standards ever since the ancient times. It is recognized as such by most nations in the world as well as being a bird that is shown respect by the same. It has influenced men throughout the ages, both good and bad; men such as Napoleon, King Arthur, as well as Adolph Hitler. Men and women throughout history have been influenced and inspired by this magnificent bird more than any other.

The United States Emblem

The American Bald Eagle became the national emblem of the United States of America by an act of Congress in 1782. Benjamin Franklin wanted the turkey to be the national emblem because he thought the eagle to represent bad moral character. Franklin also thought the turkey was more stable than the eagle. However, when it came down to the vote, the founding fathers selected the eagle as the national emblem because it is the only species of eagle that can be found in the United States. They also felt like this magnificent bird evoked courage and strength in the heart of the nation. The face of the eagle even began to be printed on certain U.S. currency. Even to this day the face of an eagle is printed on the back of a one dollar bill.

Great Britain

Great Britain still anoints their monarchs out of a vase that is in the shape of an eagle. The eagle vase is lifted above the monarch's head as oil pours from the beak of the eagle to anoint the queen or king. This has been a ritual that has been carried out since the 1400s.

Native Americans

The Native Americans still do an "eagle dance" and the eagle is still a very powerful symbol for them. The Native Americans have used eagle feathers to trade with other tribes for centuries. They have regarded the feathers as more important and valuable than those of any other bird that is alive.

The feathers are worn on the headdress and in the hair of some of the braves; distinguishing them and marking them with a higher rank and more courage than their peers. Only braves who performed deeds of fearlessness were allowed to wear the feathers in their headdress' so others would know what they had done. Nearly every tribe of Native Americans kept eagle feathers on hand for this very purpose. They never killed the eagles because they believe that would bring a great curse on their tribe. However, they did keep the majestic bird in captivity so they could have an endless supply of feathers on hand for such purposes.

Recovery Of The Bald Eagle

Perhaps one of the most powerful accomplishments of an eagle that is known in history is the recovery of the North American Bald Eagle. This bird has an extraordinary story of recovery and comeback in the face of extinction. In 1963, there were only a little over four hundred known breeding pair of eagles in the lower forty-eight states. They were placed on the endangered species list nearly ten years later. Because of the rapid decline in breeding bald eagle pairs, the banning of DDT, which is an insecticide for crops, and prohibition against hunting eagles increased the known breeding pairs of eagles to about five thousand, and over twenty thousand single eagles in the lower forty-eight states. The Bald Eagle has since been removed from the endangered species list in 1995 and is now only classified as threatened.

Even though the Bald Eagle wasn't on the brink of extinction in Alaska, they have rapidly been on the increase as well. There are now over thirty-five thousand Bald Eagles in Alaska alone! The Bald Eagle is the only eagle with a presence in every state of the United Sates except Hawaii.

Not only has this bird been important throughout history, God thought it was very important too. Now let us look at how God uses eagles as a symbol of imagery throughout the entire Bible. We are going to look at a Biblical overview of eagles throughout the Scripture, and then we're going to focus on two particular aspects of the eagle in Scripture, namely, how they represent God and how they represent man.

CHAPTER FIVE

Eagles Throughout Scripture

WITHOUT QUESTION, THE IMPORTANCE OF THE EAGLE IS TRACED throughout history. It has influenced numerous cultures and societies. The importance of the eagle is also revealed throughout the entire Bible. It is almost as if the eagle has a common thread that can be seen throughout both the Old Testament and the New Testament. It is not until you start to study these birds that you see how much they are used throughout the Bible.

Often, God uses the majestic appearance and awesome skills of the eagle to symbolize important truths for His people. God continually uses the imagery of this bird to teach us about Himself, as well as teaching us about our own lives. We are going to look at a brief overview of the eagle as it is revealed throughout the Bible.

As I've said before, there are over thirty-two references in the entire Bible to eagles. Twenty-eight out of those thirty-two references are contained in the Old Testament alone. The other four references to eagles are respectively, in the New Testament. This means that ninety percent of the references to eagles in the Bible are contained in the Old Testament alone, while only about ten percent of the references are in the New Testament. Clearly,

the Old Testament believers understood the imagery and importance of an eagle and how it was to impact their lives.

Throughout the books of Leviticus and Deuteronomy, God
lays out rules for the Israelites, telling them what they could and
could not eat. These foods were ceremonially clean and unclean
for them to consume in their daily lives. Contained within these
two books are references to eagles being unclean birds that the
Israelites were not allowed to eat. It was a forbidden bird to eat
because it was regarded as "an abomination among the birds"
(Leviticus 11:13). This doesn't mean God doesn't value the eagle, but they are just a bird that was considered unclean, so it
was not to be eaten. It is interesting that it was illegal for the Israelites to eat eagles. This is a picture for us as Christians not to
devour our own kind through backbiting and gossip.

Agur, the author of Proverbs 30, said there were only four
things that were too wonderful for him to understand. The "way
of an eagle in the air" is the first one he mentions. He says,

> There are three things which are too wonderful for me,
> Yes, four which I do not understand:
> The way of an eagle in the air,
> The way of a serpent on a rock,
> The way of a ship in the midst of the sea,
> And the way of a man with a virgin.
> (vs. 18-19)

Agur is a man who wrote one of the chapters of Proverbs and is known for his outstanding wisdom; yet he couldn't understand these four things in his lifetime. The "way of an eagle in the air" is the first one that he mentions that is beyond his understanding. He must have been just as captivated by the sight of an eagle flying through the air as we are today.

God warns that a rebellious youth attacks destructive companions as flesh draws hungry eagles to it. Agur, goes on to say in the same chapter,

> The eye that mocks his father,
> And scorns obedience to his mother,
> The ravens of the valley will pick it out,
> And the young eagles will eat it.
> (Proverbs 30:17)

God says that if we pursue riches above Him, then they will pass away as quickly as an eagle flies. God explained that a man who puts his trust in riches would see them "fly away as an eagle toward heaven" (Proverbs 23:5). The rich man's wealth will be anticipated when trouble comes just as the updrafts of the storm carries the eagle out of sight.

The strength of eagles' wings is used symbolically throughout the Bible to speak of God's swift and speedy deliverance of His people. The Children of Israel were sold into slavery and were harshly oppressed by the Egyptians for over four hundred years. They continually cried out to God and He heard them each time they lifted up their voices to Him. But when it was time for them to be delivered, just as God promised beforehand, God used the imagery of an eagle to refer to Himself delivering them from the Egyptians grip.

Three months after they were delivered, God reminded them of His quick deliverance by calling their attention back to the imagery of the eagle. He said, "You have seen what I did to the Egyptians, and how I bore you on eagles' wings and brought you to Myself" (Exodus 19:4). Not only is this referring to their swift deliverance, but also God is pictured as an eagle that is inviting them to a new level of intimacy and security with Him.

> Do not overwork to be rich; Because of your own understanding, cease! Will you set your eyes on that which is not? For riches certainly make themselves wings; They fly away like an eagle toward heaven.
>
> Proverbs 23:4-5

In addition, in Revelation 12 John tells the story of when the dragon was persecuting the woman who gave birth to the male Child. John says God gave the woman "two wings of a great eagle, that she might fly into the wilderness to her place, where she is nourished..." (Revelation 12:14). Most believe that this woman is symbolic for the Church in the End-Times. Friends, God is about to give His Church wings like an eagle so we can fly to the shelter of God and be nourished and fed by Him in the secret place.

Furthermore, the eagle also illustrates how God makes us grow up and trust completely in Him for everything we need. He is the One that leads us wherever we need to go; He will give us everything that we'll ever need in life as well. Moses reminds the Israelites of God's deliverance from Egyptian bondage when they are about to enter the Promise Land:

> As an eagle stirs up its nest,
>
> Hovers over its young,
>
> Spreading out its wings, taking them up,
>
> Carrying them on its wings,
>
> So the LORD alone led him,
>
> And there was no foreign god with him.
>
> (Deuteronomy 32:11-12)

Job uses the swiftness of an eagle catching its prey to illustrate the brevity of life. In the midst of Job's friends persecuting him, he is telling them his life is passing him by faster than he ever thought with nothing good taking place in each day. He felt like his life was just wasting away with nothing productive coming out of it. Job uses the imagery of an eagle to explain how he feels. He said,

> Now my days are swifter than a runner,
>
> They flee away, they see no good.
>
> They pass by like swift ships,
>
> Like an eagle swooping on its prey.
>
> (Job 9:25-26)

David uses the speed of an eagle to demonstrate Saul and Jonathan's skill as warriors. In lamenting their deaths, David refers to Saul and Jonathan as "beloved and pleasant in their lives", and how they were together when they died. Then David uses the king of the air and the king of the ground, namely the eagle and the lion, to illustrate their skill as warriors (see 2 Samuel 1:23).

Obviously, lions are regarded for their strength and eagles are regarded for their swiftness and speed. David was referring

> They were swifter
> than eagles,
> They were stronger
> than lions.
> 2 Samuel 1:23

to their strength and swiftness in their death. They had the strength of lions and the swiftness and speed of eagles. How valiant Saul and Jonathan must have been for David to compare them to the two animals that rule the air and ground. He uses an imagery of an eagle in their deaths!

Repeatedly, God warned His people on numerous occasions that if they persisted in evil, He would send armies against them and that He would be "as swift as the eagle flies" in judgment (Deuteronomy 28:49). He was using the swift flight of an eagle to show how fast He could cause another nation to rise up in judgment against the Israelites.

Hosea is told to proclaim the word of the Lord like a trumpet, shouting aloud and not holding back. He was to do this because the Lord was coming in judgment "like an eagle against the house of the Lord" (Hosea 8:1). He is coming swiftly, with power and might against the house of the Lord.

Throughout the Bible there seems to be the pride and haughtiness of nations rising up against God. The fact that an eagle builds its nest on the highest place of a cliff or tree is used as a picture of the foolishness of pride. Jeremiah seems to echo Ezekiel's judgment on Edom (see Ezekiel 17:3, 17) and refers to their pride and the deception of their heart when he says, "Though you make your nest on high as the eagle, I will bring you down from there" (Jeremiah 49:16). He then says God will come and "fly like an eagle, And spread His wings over

> Bless the LORD, O my soul;
> And all that is within me,
> bless His holy name! Bless the
> LORD, O my soul, And forget
> not all His benefits: Who for-
> gives all your iniquities, Who
> heals all your diseases, Who
> redeems your life from de-
> struction, Who crowns you
> with lovingkindness and ten-
> der mercies, Who satisfies
> your mouth with good
> things, So that your youth is
> renewed like the eagle's.
>
> Psalm 103:1-5

Bozrah; The heart of the mighty men of Edom in that day shall be Like the heart of a woman in birth pangs" (Jeremiah 49:22).

Both Ezekiel and John saw eagles when they had some prophetic experiences and visions (Ezekiel 1:10, 10:14; Revelation 4:7-11). The face of an eagle is used to describe one of the four living creatures that are continually worshipping around the throne of God night and day.

Jesus refers to eagles when talking about the great tribulation that is going to take place in the End-Times. He is referring the time when He would return, the time when false prophets would arise, the possibility of the deception of the elect, and all the wars breaking out, before He comes back for His own. He mentions His return will be like lightning flashing from one end of heaven to the other, so quick one will not be able to prepare for it or know when it is coming. Then He makes this statement: "For wherever the carcass is, there the eagles will be gathered together" (Matthew 24:28).

The ability of the eagle to overcome the law of gravity by stretching out its wings in flight is an important analogy of the Christian's ability to rise above the law of sin by entering into Christ's victory and by engrafting God's Word into his soul:

> But those who wait on the LORD
> Shall renew their strength;
> They shall mount up with wings like eagles,
> They shall run and not be weary,
> They shall walk and not faint.
> (Isaiah 40:31)

The eagle also speaks of the rejuvenation that is possible for all who place their faith and trust in God alone. David writes in the Psalms that we are not to forget all the benefits the Lord provides "so that [our] youth is renewed like the eagle's" (Psalm 103:5).

As you can see, a brief overview of the eagle throughout the Bible is very overwhelming and more numerous than one could have imagined. Maybe you have never seen the eagle throughout the Scripture like this. God has a lot to teach us through this magnificent bird. If you would like to do a further study on eagles as revealed in Scripture, I have included a comprehensive list in Appendix A of all the Scriptures that mention an eagle.

Even though the eagle is portrayed throughout the Bible and illustrates so many different things, there are two important aspects that we want to focus on in the next couple of chapters. In the next chapter, we are going to look more closely at how God portrays Himself as an eagle that brings freedom and liberty to those He delivers. Then, we are going to specifically focus on how God likens believers to eagles throughout the Bible.

CHAPTER SIX

The Eagle Portrays God

THE EAGLE PORTRAYS GOD MORE THAN ANY OTHER BIRD IN THE Scripture or throughout history. It is an example of God's strength, beauty, solemnity, majesty, fearlessness, and His freedom. There are two specific passages of Scripture I want us to look at in in the next two chapters from the writings of Moses that make reference to the eagle. Even though there are many other Scriptures that mention God in relation to eagles, these two in specific give us the clearest picture of how God is represented and likens Himself as an eagle.

I want to look at them in their larger contexts because I believe that we can get the greatest impact on our lives only when we fully understand the setting in which they occurred. In order for us to know what this passage actually means to us today, we must know what it meant to those to whom it was first written. I don't know about you, but I want to have the Word of God impact my life in the fullest way possible. If we know the circumstances in which God is speaking, then the impact will be more significant when we hear it.

Let us take a look at what God has to say about Himself being likened to an eagle. Prepare your heart to learn some powerful truths that will change your life.

Wilderness Experience

A careful reading of Exodus 19:1-6 suggests the eagle is symbolic of the speed of God's deliverance and redemption of the Children of Israel from Egypt. In my opinion, it is one of the greatest passages in the Bible that relates God to an eagle.

Three months after the children of Israel were delivered from Egypt, God brought them to the Wilderness of Sinai. This was the place were God was going to meet with His people in a very special way. God was getting ready to give His people the Ten Commandments (see Exodus 19-20) and reveal Himself to them in ways they had never before known. God was getting ready to manifest His glory. When God actually showed up in His glory as He promised, "Mount Sinai was completely in smoke, because the LORD descended upon it in fire" (Exodus 19:18). What a magnificent sight to behold! The mountain is descended upon by a thick cloud and it is completely covered in smoke because of the Lord's presence coming among His people. It was also at this mountain where the people of God heard His actual, audible voice for the first time!

> "'You have seen what I did to the Egyptians, and how I bore you on eagles' wings and brought you to Myself. Now therefore, if you will indeed obey My voice and keep My covenant, then you shall be a special treasure to Me above all people; for all the earth is Mine. And you shall be to Me a kingdom of priests and a holy nation.' These are the words which you shall speak to the children of Israel."
>
> Exodus 19:4-6

But before this took place, it was just an ordinary wilderness to the Israelites. Have you ever been to the wilderness? It is the place where there seems as if there is no one around to help you in your relationship with God. It seems as if everything that could go wrong is going wrong in every area of your life. We often think of the wilderness as somewhere where God's presence is not felt or experienced. We often view the wilderness with a negative perspective. There is always a wilderness experience before God takes you to the mountaintop to reveal His glory in a greater measure.

However, the wilderness is where God wants you to go so He can speak to you without any other distractions in your life. It is the place where you will hear the voice of your Father and not the voice of another speaking with you. It is the solitary place where the voice of the world is drowned out and the voice of your Father becomes very clear. It seems as if it is the only voice you hear. Jesus likens Himself to a shepherd that leads His sheep; "and the sheep follow him, for they know his voice. Yet they will by no means follow a stranger, but will flee from him, for they do not know the voice of strangers" (John 10:4-5).

God takes us into the wildness so we learn to trust Him completely with every area of our lives. It is the place where we learn greater intimacy with the Father and trust completely in Him for every need in our life. Even though God takes us into the wilderness to speak to us without the surrounding distractions, He will often get us there through pain and suffering. We get to the wilderness by not hearing His voice, where you don't feel much of His presence, where finances seem to dry up, and all our friends seem to forsake us. Have you ever been there?

God longs to have a Bride that is completely dependent on Him for everything in their lives. He wants a Bride that leans completely on Him. Song of Solomon captures this thought when the question is asked "Who is this coming up from the wilderness, Leaning upon her beloved?" (Song of Solomon 8:4). We go into the wilderness so that we come back leaning on Him with our entire lives.

A Call To Wholehearted Devotion

Hosea understood the purpose of the wilderness in his day when he declared the words of God to the wayward people. Israel had been rebellious for some time; they wouldn't turn back with wholehearted devotion to God. They wanted to have God and so much of the world at the same time. They would be described today as having a foot on both sides of the fence. God desired their wholehearted devotion to Him. He was jealous for their affections. So, God raised up Hosea to be a living message to the Israelites about how passionate the Lord is for His wayward people. Hosea's wife was a prostitute and she went to other lovers while being married to Hosea. In the same way, Israel was following other lovers when God had a marriage covenant with them.

Here, God revels His plan on how to get Israel passionate about Him once again without the distraction of other lovers: "Therefore, behold, I will allure her, Will bring her into the wilderness, And speak comfort to her" (Hosea 2:14). God draws us to Himself in the wilderness, He woos us, He entices us, and attracts us to Himself. We would not go to the wilderness willingly if we knew the pain that was going to be involved getting there. That is why God has to allure us, and in a positive sense, seduce us to come to Him in that place.

It is only in the wilderness where God speaks "comfort to her" (2:4). Do you need to be comforted today? The marginal reading of the New King James Version for speaking "comfort" to Israel, says the purpose of being led into the wilderness is so that God can "speak to her heart" – that is, Israel's heart. Beloved, God wants to speak to your heart today in the wilderness experience you are presently going through. No matter how you feel today, God hasn't forgotten you where you don't feel much of God's presence. He is wooing you so that you become more intimate with and passionate about Him.

God Is Passionate About His People

God's desire in the wilderness for the Israelites was the same as it is for us today. God delivered His people from the cruel bondage and hard oppressions so that they would worship God out in the wilderness (see Exodus 7:16; 8:1, 20; 9:1, 13; 10:3 NIV). The Israelites were delivered with a purpose. If you would ask most people in the Church today, what that purpose was, they would probably say it was to get to the Promised Land. However, that was not God's ultimate goal in delivering them from bondage. The New International Version is very clear when it says that the people are to go into the wilderness so they could "worship God." God's ultimate purpose in deliverance is to take us to a higher place of worship and a greater level of intimacy with our Father.

Furthermore, God's plan in delivering the Israelites from

> Then say to him, 'The LORD, the God of the Hebrews, has sent me to say to you: 'Let my people go, so that they may worship me in the desert. But until now you have not listened.'"
> Exodus 7:16 NIV

Egyptian bondage was so that He could bring them to Himself and dwell among them. "And they shall know that I am the LORD their God, who brought them up out of the land of Egypt, that I may dwell among them" (Exodus 29:46). God was jealous for His people. He longed to have unhindered intimacy with them once again like He did with Adam and Eve in the Garden of Eden.

A promise Paul gives in the New Testament and is found in the book of 2 Corinthians echoes what God is saying to the Israelites. It is perhaps one of the greatest promises the Lord makes to believers in the New Testament of the nearness of His presence. Paul says we are the temple of God, and because of this,

> I will dwell in them
> And walk among them.
> I will be their God,
> And they shall be My people.
> (2 Corinthians 6:16)

God never takes us into the wilderness and leaves us by ourselves. That is sometimes what it feels like to us – a very lonely place. Maybe that is what you feel like today. The fact is that we feel lonely because we're not surrounded by the busy-ness we're so used to. God will always be with us and everything He does to us is for the purpose of bringing us closer to Himself. He is jealous for our time and affection.

God's Covenant

After they had been brought out of Egypt and traveled for about three months, they "camped there before the mountain" (Exodus 19:2). The mountain they camped at the foot of was none other than Mt. Sinai. It is the same as the "mountain of God," which is also called Horeb, where Moses had the powerful experience with God at the burning bush (Exodus 3:1; 4:27; 18:5, 24:13).

Throughout the Bible, Moses frequently goes to this mountain to receive revelation from the Lord and it is the place he takes the Israelites to meet with God. We, as ministers of the new covenant, must learn to go to the mountain of God. Because of our leadership gifting, we will draw others to us and we can even have successful ministries and big churches. Nevertheless, this can be accomplished with our personal gifting and charisma – without ever going to the mountain to meet with God. It is God's desire and intention for us to meet with Him on the mountain. We must learn from Moses who spent much of his time on the mountain before he spent time in front of the people.

Moses went up into the presence of God to meet with Him on the mountain while the rest of the children of Israel stayed at the foot of the mountain. The Israelites *played* church while Moses was *doing* church and meeting with God in the thick cloud. As Moses was meeting with God, "the LORD called to him from the mountain" (vs. 3). God called Moses' name and gave him an invitation to experience the presence of the Lord in a greater measure than what he was presently experiencing.

As Moses drew near in intimacy, God spoke to Moses something that he was to repeat to the Children of Israel. In this spoken oracle was contained the imagery of an eagle. Here is what God said:

> You have seen what I did to the Egyptians, and how I bore you on eagles' wings and brought you to Myself. Now therefore, if you will indeed obey My voice and keep My covenant, then you shall be a special treasure to Me above all people; for all the earth is Mine. And you shall be to

Me a kingdom of priests and a holy nation.
(Exodus 19:4-6)

In this passage, God is calling the Israelites back into covenant with Him. But before He does this, He recalls their attention to two acts that He has performed for them to bring their hearts and minds back into focus.

First, He recalls their attention to the judgments He has recently poured out on the Egyptians as He led the Children of Israel out of Egyptian bondage. These judgments are the revealing of the Lord's passionate and burning heart for His people. Because He loved them and was so passionate about them, He was going to do anything to get the affections and emotions of their heart solely focused on Him once again. God was going to achieve His goal, even if He had to pour out judgments on an entire wicked nation because of the hardness of one man's heart, namely Pharaoh.

The second act He calls their attention to is the fact that He brought the Israelites to Himself by bearing them on eagles' wings. God was calling them to Himself – He was drawing them near using the imagery of an eagle. God was so passionate about His people that He couldn't stand any longer to see them in slavery and to be treated unjustly. So, He compares Himself to an eagle that swooped down and bore them, or sustained them, on the wings of an eagle to bring them out of the land of Egypt. It wasn't just to bring them out of somewhere; it was to bring them to Someone. God brought them out of Egypt and carried them to Himself.

Bore Them On Eagles' Wings

God said that he bore them on eagles' wings and brought them to Himself. The word "bore" in the Hebrew text is used over 650 times throughout the entire Old Testament. It has a number of definitions, but is defined by Vine's Expository Dictionary as "to remove, depart, and carry away."[ii] The first occurrence of this word in the Bible is in Genesis 7:17 where it is reported that the waters "lifted up" the ark when God made it rain and flooded the earth.

This same word is applied to marriage, or taking a wife to oneself (Ruth 1:4). This is used when Naomi's sons took wives from the women of Moab. How prophetic is this when God "bore them on eagles' wings" and brought them to Himself. In essence, He was entering into a marriage covenant with them. The biggest covenant of all that God talks about and uses as a symbol for Himself in the Bible is the marriage covenant. God was entering into a marriage covenant with the Israelites as He brought them out of the land of Egypt.

[ii] Vine, W.E., and Merril Unger, and William White, Jr. *Vines Complete Expository Dictionary Of Old and New Testament Words.* (Nashville, TN: Thomas Nelson, Inc., 1984), 200-201.

So how does the word "bore" carry over into the natural realm? Well, as we've learned earlier, an eagle will swoop down under its young until it learns to fly on its own. This is an amazing picture of what God did with the Israelites. The judgments of God poured out on Egypt and how He bore Israel on eagles' wings are the two acts of God that the Israelites' attention is called to before God draws them into covenant relationship with Himself.

For the blessings of this covenant to take effect, God said the Israelites would have to "obey My voice" and "keep My covenant." If they will do the two requirements the Lord asks of them, then He will make them a "special treasure to Me above all people" and He will make them a "kingdom of priests and a holy nation."

The Lord's Special Treasure

The promise of being the Lord's special treasure is fulfilled in the New Testament in the first epistle of Peter. Peter declares in direct reference to Exodus 19:

> But you are a chosen generation, a royal priesthood, a holy nation, His own special people, that you may proclaim the praises of Him who called you out of darkness into His marvelous light; who were once not a people but are now the people of God, who had not obtained mercy but now have obtained mercy. (1 Peter 2:9-10)

The theme of the people of God being a "special treasure" is a theme that runs throughout the whole of the Bible. With almost every instance of people "being the LORD's special treasure," it also says the "LORD chose" them to be that special treasure. With being the Lord's treasure, there is also a measure that the Lord chooses us for that position. Holding this position before God distinguishes us from everyone else on the face of the earth. Let me give you a few Scriptures that illustrate this principle.

Moses tells the Israelites twice before they enter the Promise Land that they area chosen and special treasure.

> For you are a holy people to the LORD your God; **the LORD your God has chosen you to be a people for Himself, a special treasure above all the peoples on the face of the earth.** The LORD did not set His love on you nor choose you because you were more in number than any other people, for you were the least of all peoples; but because the LORD loves you, and because He would keep the oath which He swore to your fathers, the LORD has brought you out with a mighty hand, and redeemed you from the house of bondage, from the hand of Pharaoh king of Egypt. (Deuteronomy 7:6-8, Emphasis mine)

And again,

> This day the LORD your God commands you to
> observe these statutes and judgments; therefore
> you shall be careful to observe them with all your
> heart and with all your soul. Today you have pro-
> claimed the LORD to be your God, and that you will
> walk in His ways and keep His statutes, His com-
> mandments, and His judgments, and that you will
> obey His voice. Also today **the LORD has pro-
> claimed you to be His special people**, just as He
> promised you, that you should keep all His com-
> mandments, and that He will set you high above
> all nations which He has made, in praise, in name,
> and in honor, and that you may be a holy people to
> the LORD your God, just as He has spoken. (Deu-
> teronomy 26:16-19, Emphasis mine)

The Psalmist knew and understood the same principle
of being the Lord's treasure and being chosen when he
declared,

> Praise the Lord!
> Praise the name of the Lord;
> Praise Him, O you servants of the Lord!
> You who stand in the house of the Lord,
> In the courts of the house of our God,
> Praise the Lord, for the Lord is good;
> Sing praises to His name, for it is pleasant.

**For the Lord has chosen Jacob for Himself,
Israel for His special treasure**.
(Psalm 135:1-4, Emphasis mine)

And Malachi ties the same theme together when he says,

"They shall be Mine," says the Lord of hosts,
"On the day that **I make them My jewels [or, special treasure]**.
And I will spare them
As a man spares his own son who serves him."
(Malachi 3:17, Emphasis mine)

Friends, clearly from the Word of God, you are a chosen vessel; the Lord's own special treasure above all peoples on the face of the earth. God has bore you on eagles' wings and delivered you from the bondage of the world; from the effects of sin and unrighteousness in your life. He delivered you so that He could draw you into a deeper relationship with Himself. It wasn't so you could inherit the Promise Land like most think today. It was so that He could bring you to Himself and His presence could dwell with you and be in you.

God's Mercy In Deliverance

When Isaiah is speaking of the mercy of God, and calling the Children of Israel to remember it as well, he speaks of God's mercy being shown in their deliverance from Egyptian bondage.

When Isaiah is calling their mind and heart back to this incident, he uses the same language God used when He said that He "bore them on eagles' wings" in their deliverance from Egypt (see Exodus 19:4).

Isaiah prophesies this:

I will mention the lovingkindnesses of the Lord
And the praises of the Lord,
According to all that the Lord has bestowed on
     us,
And the great goodness toward the house of
     Israel,
Which He has bestowed on them according to
     His mercies,
According to the multitude of His
     lovingkindnesses.
For He said, "Surely they are My people,
Children who will not lie."
So He became their Savior.
In all their affliction He was afflicted,
And the Angel of His Presence saved them;
In His love and in His pity He redeemed them;
And He bore them and carried them
All the days of old.
But they rebelled and grieved His Holy Spirit;
So He turned Himself against them as an
     enemy,

77

And He fought against them.

(Isaiah 63:7-10, Emphasis mine)

When the Prophet Isaiah says, "He bore them and carried them", he is referring to when the Lord took Israel out of Egypt to bring them to Himself. Even though this was one act of God, it was perhaps the most significant event in the entire history of Israel. The only other event that would surpass the Exodus would be the coming of Jesus as the Messiah to save His people.

Can see how passionate the Lord is about you? He uses the imagery of an eagle swooping down to get its young as a picture for His deliverance of your life from the ways of the world. God was so in love with you that He could not leave you where you where at in your present condition. He had to rescue you and deliver you from everything that was limiting your potential and destiny in Him.

CHAPTER SEVEN

God Stirs The Nest

THE SECOND PASSAGE I WOULD LIKE TO DEAL WITH IN REGARDS to God likening Himself to an eagle comes also from the writings of Moses. In fact, it is even a reference to the Israelites deliverance from the bondage of Egypt. However, this time the imagery is used almost forty years later to recall to the people's hearts and minds all that God had done for them up until that point.

After God delivered the Children of Israel from the bondage of Egypt, Moses led them through the wilderness for forty years because of their disobedience. After seeing God provide for them for forty years by miracles, signs and wonders, they finally came to the edge of the river where they saw their inheritance – the Promise Land. Everyone must have been so excited because this is their first glimpse of what only has been talked about and dreamed about up until this point. This is what they had been waiting such a long time for. Finally, they were at the edge of the river looking at their inheritance – the promise of God. They could see it! It produced worship in them to recount what God had done in their lives throughout the time they left Egypt until the present.

Standing on the rivers edge, Moses begins to sing a song to everyone in Israel recalling to mind all the works the Lord had done for them throughout this powerful wilderness experience of the past forty years (see Deuteronomy 32:1).

In referring to Jacob, which is another way of referring to the Israelites, Moses said that God had found him in a wilderness and wasteland. When God saw him, "He encircled him, He instructed him, He kept him as the apple of His eye" (vs. 10). He then says goes on to say:

> As an eagle stirs up its nest,
>
> Hovers over its young,
>
> Spreading out its wings, taking them up,
>
> Carrying them on its wings,
>
> So the LORD alone led [Jacob, or the Israelites],
>
> And there was no foreign god with him.
>
> [vs. 11-12, Brackets mine]

To show that it was the Lord alone who led the Children of Israel out of Egypt and through the desert, and a foreign god was not with them, God gave them the imagery of an eagle again to portray this powerful truth. The eagle is here speaking of God's wise and loving parental care of His children.

Learning To Fly

In the natural, when an eagle is building its nest, it will line it with sharp rocks and thorns. Then the mother eagle will place the fur and hair of animals that have been killed over the rough bottom. This is so that the nest will be very comfortable and cozy

for the eaglet to be born into. But when it comes time for the eaglets to fly on their own, the mother eagle will do a few things to
teach them how to fly.

First, she will hover about three to four feet above the nest to
demonstrate to her eaglets that they are able to fly. Eagles,
though large birds, have a similar ability that a humming bird
has. They have the ability to hover in one spot for long periods of
time. Though they don't flap their wings like hummingbirds do –
eagles catch an air current and are able to suspend almost mo-
tionless for a brief time so the eaglets can see that their wings
are able to do the same.

Next, she will remove the fur and hair so it will not be comfortable for the young eagle to stay in the nest any longer. The
sharp rocks and thorns thrust the eaglet out to try to fly on its
own. The eaglet will go to the edge of the nest and peer over to
the ground far below. If the eaglet doesn't voluntarily try to fly on
its own, then the mother eagle will help it fly with a little nudge off
the edge of the nest.

The mother eagle will let the eaglet almost hit the ground
before she will swoop under it and pick it back up again on her
wings. Then she will fly very high and drop it again doing the
same thing before it hits the ground. She will do this repeatedly
until the eaglet struggles to flap its wings and learns to fly on its
own. It is interesting that the young eagles are three to four
months of age by the time this begins to take place, which

means they are nearly full grown before they have to try and fly on their own.

Even after she does this with the eaglet in flying, the mother continues to be by its side to aid it in the flying process for some time. She continues to gently aid it with her wings to help stabilize its flying until it gets better at flying on its own. Eventually, the mother won't aid the eaglet anymore because it has matured and learned to soar on its own. This is very similar to what God does to us.

God Stirs Our Nest

It is the longing of God's heart that He teaches us to fly and soar on the wings of eagles. It was never God's intention for the Israelites to stay in Egypt the rest of their life. God had a plan and purpose for them. They were created for so much more! They were created to leave the bondage of Egypt and draw near to God in true intimacy and fellowship.

Even though the Children of Israel were in bondage, God still had to "stir the nest" to get them to want to leave. Sure, they cried out to the Lord for deliverance the whole time they were there. However, as you can see from later incidents, they were comfortable there. After they heard the report of the twelve spies who went to spy out the Promised Land, they lifted up their voices and lamented because they didn't die in Egypt. In fact, they even wanted to appoint another leader to take them back to the place where they were comfortable, namely, to the land of Egypt (see Numbers 14:1-4). God had to stir Israel's nest in order to get them to leave Egypt. Israel never would have left on their own without God prodding them to move on. They were comfortable and satisfied there even though Egypt was corrupt and wicked.

God must stir our nest occasionally as well to get us to move from the place of being comfortable. Sure, it was never our intention to be comfortable. It just seems to happen over time if we are not continually seeking the face of God. God's desire is not for us to be in a place of comfortableness, but to be in a place of pure passion for Him. If we sit in our comfortable place for too long, then God will suddenly stir the nest so we are awakened for what we are destined for. He loves us too much and has too big of a plan for our life for us to just sit and waste it away.

Showing Us The Way

When an eagle is "hovering over its young," it is not doing it as a protective measure as we would first think. No, the mother eagle hovers over its young to show it what it was created for. She does it so the eaglet will see what it is able to do with its wings. She is showing the eaglet that it has the same potential that she does, if it will just use its wings.

In the same way, the Father didn't leave us alone when it comes to living life. In fact, He gave us the ultimate *eagle be-*

liever so we would know how to live life. Jesus came as the ultimate expression of the Father. The author of Hebrews says that Jesus is "the brightness of [the Father's] glory and the express image of His person" (Hebrews 1:3).

In fact, Jesus said that if you had seen Him, you had seen the Father also. When Jesus was speaking of His departure, Philip asked Him, "Lord, show us the Father, and it is sufficient for us." Then Jesus replied to him by saying, "Have I been with you so long, and yet you have not known Me, Philip? He who has seen Me has seen the Father; so how can you say, 'Show us the Father'? Do you not believe that I am in the Father, and the Father in Me? The words that I speak to you I do not speak on My own authority; but the Father who dwells in Me does the works. Believe Me that I am in the Father and the Father in Me, or else believe Me for the sake of the works themselves" (John 14:8-11).

If we have seen Jesus, then we know who the Father is. God didn't leave us alone. But, through Jesus, He has showed us that we are created for so much more than just a "normal Christian life." We are able to do the same things Jesus did because we have the Holy Spirit dwelling on the inside of us.

God stirs up our nest and hovers over us to show us that there is so much more that we are able to do through His power and might than what we are presently experiencing. If we are not living the same way Jesus did, then there is still more for us to be experiencing in this life.

God Sustains Us

As we begin to step out and walk this God-kind of life, it is nice to know that God has not left us alone. He showed us the way through the life and ministry of Jesus, and now He helps us live that life through the power of the Holy Spirit. Jesus said that we would receive power when the Holy Spirit came upon us (see Acts 1:8). Now that we have the Holy Spirit upon us and within us, we are able to live in the same power of the Spirit that Jesus did.

> And being assembled together with them, He commanded them not to depart from Jerusalem, but to wait for the Promise of the Father, "which," He said, "you have heard from Me; for John truly baptized with water, but you shall be baptized with the Holy Spirit not many days from now...But you shall receive power when the Holy Spirit has come upon you; and you shall be witnesses to Me in Jerusalem, and in all Judea and Samaria, and to the end of the earth."
>
> Acts 1:4-5, 8

Even after the eaglet is thrust out of the nest, the mother eagle will continue to fly to help stabilize and sustain the eaglet in flight. In the same way, once we are born again, God is right there stabilizing us and helping us to walk just like Jesus walked. It is not something we have to attain to on our own. Through the Holy Spirit, God is continually with us helping us to live the type of life that Jesus lived.

The Israelites had to learn to trust the Lord completely with their lives. They had to learn to be carried on the wings of the Lord and rely completely on them to come fully out of bondage. This was not something that was to be mastered in a couple of weeks. In fact, they stayed in the wilderness for forty years because they didn't trust the things that He had spoken to them.

Friends, let us learn to trust God through every season of our life. He is continually watching over us and right beside us as we go through life. Even if you don't sense His nearness like you once did, He is still there. Hebrews 13:5, in The Amplified Bible, is one of the most emphatic verses contained in the entire Bible about God's nearness to us. It says, "for He [God] Himself has said, I will not in any way fail you nor give you up nor leave you without support. [I will] not, [I will] not, [I will] not in any degree leave you helpless nor forsake nor let [you] down (relax My hold on you)! [Assuredly not!]" I don't think God is going to leave us through any circumstance we go through.

God Teaches Us How To Fly

We are created to fly! We are not created to sit in the comfortable nest without being stirred to fulfill our potential. God will stir up our nest until we learn to soar upon the heights with wings of eagles. God will stir up our world so that we learn to fly and press into Him. We've learned that once a week feedings are no longer sufficient to sustain our souls. We have to learn to fly on our own and learn to feed ourselves on a daily basis. We are to be fed when we attend church, but that is just to be a "booster shot" so that we dig into the Word and pray throughout the rest of the week.

Jesus is our ultimate model in life. He came to show us who the Father really is. We have now seen the Father through the life and ministry of Jesus. He has not left us alone! He has sent the Holy Spirit to be our Comforter to sustain us through every trial and tribulation we go through.

Now that we've seen how God relates Himself to an eagle, let us now look at how he likens us, as believers, to an eagle. The two main passages we are going to look at are the basis of us becoming *eagle believers*.

CHAPTER EIGHT

The Believer Likened To An Eagle

EVEN THOUGH THERE ARE MANY VERSES THROUGHOUT THE BIBLE relating the believer's life to that of an eagle, there are two passages that seem to stick out above all the rest. In this chapter, I want to examine these two passages. We will see that we, as believer's, are called to have the wings of an eagle and soar high above our earthly circumstances, or to borrow Tommy Tenney's words, we are to have "God's Eye-View"[iii] of our situation. In the same way God is portrayed as an eagle rescuing His people from disaster and destruction, the believer is portrayed as an eagle that mounts up with wings and experiences rejuvenation from the Lord.

Every so often in life, we go through a time where we don't feel very passionate about, or in love with the Lord. We are neither hot nor cold, but we're living in a place of lukewarmness (see Revelation 3:16). We know that we should be more passionate, and in fact, we really want to be. However, we don't! We don't want to work up our emotions and try to be passionate

---

[iii] This phrase is borrowed from Tommy Tenney's book entitled, *God s Eye View: Worshipping Your Way to A Higher Perspective.* (Nashville, TN: Thomas Nelson, Inc., 2002).

without a true heart response. God doesn't want us to work ourselves up either. He knows our hearts anyway; there is no use
trying to make ourselves look more passionate than we really
are.

Rejuvenation Comes From The Lord

One passage that speaks of the believer experiencing rejuvenation from the Lord is found in Psalm 103. David is speaking
to his soul and commanding it to bless and praise the Lord with
all of his inmost being – that is to put his whole heart in his praise to God. As he is telling his soul to bless the Lord, he also reminds him-self to "forget not all His benefits" (vs. 2). The word

> Five Benefits of Psalm 103
>
> 1. As A Sinner He Forgives Me
> 2. As A Sick Man He Heals Me
> 3. As A Slave He Redeems Me
> 4. As A Son He Crowns Me
> 5. As A Saint He Satisfies Me

"benefit" that is used here refers to a kindness shown or something that is an advantage or promotes well-being. Then David
goes on to list the five specific benefits the Lord gives to those
who bless or praise His name.

The first benefit that David mentions in relation to blessing
the Lord is that He forgives all of our sins – God will forgive every
sin that we have ever committed. He doesn't care what you've
done in your life; His blood is powerful enough to cleanse you
from all sin. John writes in his first epistle, "He is faithful and just

to forgive us our sins and to cleanse us from all unrighteous-ness" (1 John 1:9).

The second benefit God gives us is that He heals all of our diseases – God reveals Himself as the "the LORD who heals you" (Exodus 15:26). He is the healer of our bodies as well as the healer of our spiritual sicknesses, namely sin. David doesn't only say that He heals some of our diseases; David says He heals *all* of our diseases. Friends, there is not one sickness or infirmity you may have that God cannot or will not heal.

The third benefit is that of redeeming our life from destruc-tion – He delivers us from death as we praise the Lord. Sure, we are going to eventually die. However, for us who have Christ in our hearts, there is life after death. We possess eternal life now, and in the age to come. This life is only temporary.

The Lord will also crown us with loving-kindness and tender mercies – God places a crown of love and compassion on us as we bless and praise Him. He enriches our life with loyal love and tender compassion as we worship Him with all of our heart.

Lastly, David says that He is the one that satisfies us with good things. Depending on what translation of the Bible you are reading, it will vary in what it is saying. The New King James says God will "fill our mouth with good things." The New Interna-tional Version says that it is He "who satisfies your desires with good things." Lastly, and the one that I chose is what the English Standard Version has to say. It says God is the one who "satisfies you with good." I chose the last one because when *you* are satisfied with good, then your mouth and your desires will be satisfied as well. If you are satisfied with good, then everything you are is going to be satisfied also.

All of these benefits are followed by a "so that" phrase. David says the Lord gives all of these benefits to us "*So that* your youth is renewed like the eagle's" (vs. 5, Italics mine). All of these blessings are not just for the purpose of themselves, though God does give these to bless us. However, all of these blessings are for the purpose of being renewed like an eagle.

Renewed Like An Eagle

The word "renewed" in this passage means to "make new" or "to repair." God gives these five specific benefits to make us completely new or to repair parts of our lives that are broke down. If we are sick, then He repairs us with healing. If we are stuck in sin and bondage, then He repairs us with His love and forgiveness. If we are not experiencing good things in our life, then He will give us those good things that we need to experience so we have a full and satisfying life.

"Renewed" further means to "renew" or to "restore." We are not talking about being renewed or restored so you feel a little better than you did before. It is much more than that. One Hebrew Dictionary defines it as to "place in a state or condition identical or nearly the same as a prior state."[iv] This is such an amazing word so full of meaning and life! To be renewed doesn't mean that we experience these benefits in a small way. No! It is to experience the abundance of life Jesus talks about in the New Testament (see John 10:10). Whatever area God gives us His benefits in, these restore or renew us to the identical or a higher state than where we were at before.

This renewal that we experience is referred to "like the eagle's" (vs. 5). This could possibly be referring to the increase of vigor that an eagle experiences after the molting process runs its full course in its life. As described before, the eagle will go through a molting process in life where it

> The thief does not come except to steal, and to kill, and to destroy. I have come that they may have life, and that they may have it more abundantly.
> John 10:10

is stripped of everything that it previously trusted in. It plucks out its feathers, breaks off its beak, and rubs off its talons until they are left defenseless, and totally dependent upon one another. Maybe this is what the Psalmist meant – that God wanted him to experience a renewed passion toward the end of his life.

The author of Psalm 92:12-15 believes the Lord has a long, full, satisfying life for him. He says,

---

[iv] Swanson, J. (1997). *Dictionary of Biblical Languages with Semantic Domains: Hebrew (Old Testament)* (electronic ed.) (HGK2542). Oak Harbor: Logos Research Systems, Inc.

> The righteous shall flourish like a palm tree,
>
> He shall grow like a cedar in Lebanon.
>
> Those who are planted in the house of the Lord
>
> Shall flourish in the courts of our God.
>
> They shall still bear fruit in old age;
>
> They shall be fresh and flourishing,
>
> To declare that the Lord is upright;
>
> He is my rock, and there is no unrighteousness
>
> in Him.

If we are to have our youth renewed like the eagle's, then we must do the things prescribed by David *so that* we can be renewed. We must experience all of these benefits the Lord gives us before we have the fresh life and vigor which is described here. However, we cannot experience these benefits if we don't learn how to bless and praise the Lord with our entire being – our whole heart being enthralled by the praises of God.

In whatever season you are in today, begin to praise the name of the Lord and you will begin to experience these benefits. As you experience these benefits, your youth will be renewed like the eagle's.

Mounting Up With Eagles' Wings

Now let us examine the fortieth chapter of the book of Isaiah. In my opinion, this is one of the greatest promises of rest and renewal contained in the entire Bible. It is a promise of us waiting on the Lord and Him coming to renew our strength like an eagle.

It is very closely related to Psalm 103:5. As with Psalm 103:5, this could possibly be referring to the eagles' increase of vigor and life after the molting process has run its course in the later part of its life.

God is revealing to us a further revelation in Isaiah 40; building upon the Deuteronomy 32 passage. In Deuteronomy 32 God was teaching us about being stirred out of the nest and eventually learning how to fly on our own with the wind of the Holy Spirit. Isaiah 40 is not teaching us just how to fly – God is teaching us that He wants us to learn how to soar. We were not created to flap our wings and struggle to fly. However, we are created to soar in the high places with Jesus! Soaring requires resting and waiting upon the winds of the Spirit of God for our movement. Flying requires us trying in ourselves instead of trusting the winds of God to pick us up and take us to heights only He can take us to. Flying is good and it is of God. But God's ultimate purpose in our lives is to get us to soar!

Here is what Isaiah was speaking to the people of God in his generation. They were obviously tired and weary from life, resorting that God didn't see what was going on in their lives. Isaiah challenges this myth with the truth from the heart of God. He says,

> Why do you say, O Jacob,
> And speak, O Israel:
> "My way is hidden from the LORD,

And my just claim is passed over by my God"?

Have you not known?

Have you not heard?

The everlasting God, the LORD,

The Creator of the ends of the earth,

Neither faints nor is weary.

His understanding is unsearchable.

He gives power to the weak,

And to those who have no might He increases
   strength.

Even the youths shall faint and be weary,

And the young men shall utterly fall,

But those who wait on the LORD

Shall renew their strength;

They shall mount up with wings like eagles,

They shall run and not be weary,

They shall walk and not faint.

(Isaiah 40:27-31)

Here is another translation from THE MESSAGE that I believe
puts what Isaiah is saying in a way that is easier to understand
and comprehend:

"So—who is like me?

   Who holds a candle to me?" says The Holy.

Look at the night skies:

   Who do you think made all this?

Who marches this army of stars out each night,

counts them off, calls each by name
—so magnificent! so powerful!—
and never overlooks a single one?
Why would you ever complain, O Jacob,
or, whine, Israel, saying,
"GOD has lost track of me.
He doesn't care what happens to me"?
Don't you know anything? Haven't you been listening?
GOD doesn't come and go. God lasts.
He's Creator of all you can see or imagine.
He doesn't get tired out, doesn't pause to catch his breath.
And he knows everything, inside and out.
He energizes those who get tired,
gives fresh strength to dropouts.
For even young people tire and drop out,
young folk in their prime stumble and fall.
But those who wait upon GOD get fresh strength.
They spread their wings and soar like eagles,
They run and don't get tired,
they walk and don't lag behind.
(Isaiah 40:25-31, THE MESSAGE)

It is interesting Isaiah refers to the children of Israel by the inspiration of the Holy Spirit as "Jacob" and "Israel." Most likely, this is a reference to Genesis 32:22-32, when Jacob wrestled with God and gained new strength when he prevailed. God changed the name of this renewed wrestler to Israel instead of Jacob. The story of Jacob wrestling with God would surely be in the mind of all who heard this word from Isaiah.

Instead of the Israelites praising the Lord, they began to complain that God didn't know their situation or have any concern for their problems. They thought the Lord was asking them to do too much – to do the impossible in their own strength. The people were very tired and weary. They complained they didn't have enough strength for the journey. It is out of the midst of these circumstances that this amazing promise from God comes forth!

Then the Prophet reminds the people that they are worshipping and serving a God that is an "everlasting God" and "the LORD" and "The Creator of the ends of the earth." He is a God that "neither faints nor is weary" and His "understanding is unreachable." He is the One who sustains us through all of our trials and tribulations. It is He who we trust in with all of our hearts and minds. He is the One who gives "power to the weak" and to those who have no strength left in their lives, it is He who "increases strength" for them.

Isaiah then calls his reader's attention to how the young people "faint" and are "weary." The point here is that the young people, who represent life, vitality, and energy, even have a point where they can't do anymore because they are so tired and worn out. Implied in the Hebrew wording here is that these young men are the "chosen ones" that have been scouted out by the Olympics during that time period in history. That means that this is a reference to young men who are in the peak of their life when it comes to physical condition. Even they become physically, spiritually, and emotionally exhausted. Weary is referring to failure under life's pressures. Weak is literally referring to the one who has no vigor or vitality. They have a lack of innate strength. If these young men can get exhausted, then everyone is liable to get exhausted.

> Waiting means to hope for, expect, and eagerly look for the Lord to come and renew your strength. It is binding together with the Lord while you wait for Him to come and do only what He can do.

It is out of the midst of this weariness on behalf of the Lord's people that the great promise of verse 31 comes. "Those who wait on the LORD Shall renew their strength; They shall mount up with wings like eagles, They shall run and not be weary, They shall walk and not faint."

Waiting On The Lord

The promise of rest and renewal come from "waiting" on the Lord. The word "wait" in verse 31 does not mean to sit around and do nothing. It is not a passive word, as it is often understood in our culture today. We wait for a phone call, we wait at the bus stop, and we wait in line at the grocery store. We usually don't do too much while we are "waiting" for these things to take place in our life. We may look at some magazines while we "wait" in the grocery store line. We are not interested in them; we just want to fill our time until it is our turn in line. Have you ever ridden the bus? We usually "wait" without doing too much until the bus finally arrives. If you ever drive by a bus stop, you usually see people either staring off into space or reading some boring romance novel while they "wait" for the bus to come. We live a life of constant waiting. This is even true when we go to fast food restaurants so we don't have to wait as long to eat. We are still waiting.

However, the Hebrew word for "wait" is much different from

> We are to bind together in our quiet times with the Lord, becoming increasingly united with Him in our lives through intimacy.

what it means to us in our present lives. It is not a passive waiting that Isaiah is talking about – a waiting where we sit around and waste time until the waiting is over. "Wait", in this context is an action word. It means to "to wait, look for eagerly, to hope for, or to expect."

In the Hebrew culture, they usually defined words by describing a picture to illustrate the word. To define a word in the Hebrew language was not to give abstract truth, much like our modern dictionaries do, but to describe the word by using a picture. The picture for "wait" is of a three-stranded cord that is being woven or bound together very tightly. When we "wait" on the Lord, we are actually binding together continually tighter with Him in intimacy. Our love relationship with Him is continually increasing. This binding together only comes through being in His presence – this will look different to each of us individually.

It is much the same when a husband and wife come together in intimacy. The Bible states that when a man leaves his mother and father and clings to his wife that the two "shall become one flesh" (see Genesis 2:24). That is why the author of Ecclesiastes says that a "threefold cord is not easily broken" (Ecclesiastes 4:12).

We are to look to God for all that we need in life. One Hebrew Dictionary further defines it as to "look forward with confidence to that which is good and beneficial, often with a focus of anticipation in a future event."[v] Each time the object of the "hope" is the Lord, there is an eager expectation of salvation or deliverance. When we "wait" on the Lord, we are "waiting" with intense expectation for Him to come and renew us with the faithfulness of His presence.

We are called to be a people who learn to wait on the Lord in our daily lives. We are not to fill our time with things that don't matter in life while we casually wait for Him to show up. No, we are to actively pursue His presence in a passionate and intense way as we are waiting for Him to come with salvation. We are to bind together in our quiet times with the Lord, becoming increasingly united with Him in our lives through intimacy. We are to get

---

[v] Swanson, Ibid. (HGK7747).

so intertwined with the Lord that it is no longer we who are living, but Christ living His life through us.

In Isaiah's time, the people of God had an intense expectation that He was going to come in a very special way. They were waiting for the promise of the Messiah to come and deliver the people of God like it had been prophesied about for many years. They were getting tired and weary of waiting for the promise. The author of Proverbs says "hope deferred makes the heart sick, But when desire comes, it is a tree of life" (Proverbs 13:12). Isaiah tells the people who were about to give up because of their weariness to,

> Strengthen the weak hands,
> And make firm the feeble knees.
> Say to those who are fearful-hearted,
> "Be strong, do not fear!
> Behold, your God will come with vengeance,
> With the recompense of God;
> He will come and save you."
> (Isaiah 35:3-4)

Friends, no matter what your situation is today, He is coming! Don't give up on waiting for the Lord to come; He is coming. He is coming to save you and deliver you from any situation that you are in today!

As we wait on the Lord, we are going to be renewed in our strength. The word "renew" in this context, means "to exchange" as if taking off old clothes and putting on brand new clothes. This literally means to "experience an invigorated, restorative rest." It is not just a rest where we sleep and wake up physically refreshed. It is a rest that restores our spirit, soul, and body as we continue to "wait" on and bind together with the Lord. We exchange our weakness for His power (2 Corinthians 12:1-10). Warren Wiersbe says, "As we wait before Him, God enables us to soar when there is a crisis, to run when the challenges are many, and to walk faithfully in the day-by-day demands of life. It is much harder to walk in the ordinary pressures of life than to fly like the eagle in a time of crisis."[vi]

"They shall mount up with wings like eagles" literally means, "They shall put forth fresh feathers as eagles." Do you have fresh feathers today? Have you waited on the Lord with intense expectation in intimacy for Him to come? Have you waited on Him with an intense love yearning for His presence in you life? It is not too late to start. God is yearning for your attention right now.

Now that we've seen how important the eagle was throughout history and the Bible, let us turn our attention to the home f the eagle. We're going to examine how an eagle will find its mate and also how they will build a nest together. Eagles are interested in making a strong home life.

[vi] Wiersbe, W. W. (1996, c1992). *Be Comforted.* An Old Testament Study. (Is 40:1). Wheaton, Ill.: Victor Books.

CHAPTER NINE

The Eagles Home

Mating Patterns

ONE OF THE ASPECTS OF AN EAGLE BUILDING ITS HOME IS IN ITS finding a mate. Let me tell you how an eagle will find a mate, then how they will build a home together as a couple. Eagles will always build their home together – it is built by both male and female. Each one of them has an active part to play in the construction of their home.

When the eagle is a year old, it begins to take care of itself and finally leaves the security of its parent's nest. After the eagle has been on its own for about three years, it begins to take interest in a bird of the opposite sex. Spring fever comes to the eagles and they start a game of tag that often lasts for many days. The female eagle becomes bored with this game so she invents her own game. This game, however, is not her own invention because the eagle has been playing it for many centuries.

The game they play goes something like this: the female dives to the ground and grabs a stick in her talons. She takes it and flies up high with the male eagle following right behind her. When she gets eight to ten thousand feet up in the air, she drops the stick. The male dives down and picks up the stick before it hits the ground. When the potential mate catches the stick, he will bring it back up to the female hight in the air. However, the female doesn't want the stick the male retrieved for her. Then the female eagle dives and picks up another stick from the ground and begins to fly back up to the same altitude. When she reaches a certain altitude, she begins to fly a figure eight pattern with wide curves and the male eagle, with pride, stays right behind her. In this peculiar pattern, the female suddenly drops the stick again and the male, being such a gentleman, attempts to retrieve it for her by breaking the pattern, swooping down, and catching the stick. He then flies to return it to her, however, the female, seeming uninterested, dives down to the ground where there is another stick. She picks this one up and does it all over again.

Each time she repeats this, the stick gets larger and heavier. With every stick she flies lower to the ground, and the stick approaches the ground a lot faster because of the weight of the stick. The male eagle has to do more of a radical dive each time to retrieve the stick for its potential mate. If the male ever fails to catch the falling stick, the female will chase him off and never play with him again. This is a test so the male eagle proves his manhood.

The game climaxes when the female is flying at a tremendous speed in the figure eight pattern less than five hundred feet above the ground. She releases an object weighing almost as much as she weighs and when she drops it, she is expecting the male to grab the stick before it hits the ground. He has to be an incredible sportsman to be able to accomplish such a task. If the male eagle finally catches the stick, it will be very close to the ground and he will have to break out of the dive very carefully, lest he hit the ground. It is a very dangerous game.

After finally satisfying the female, the male is fit to become her husband and they start making their marriage vows. Have you ever seen on TV some of the people who get married while skydiving? They are skydiving together and minister is up there skydiving performing the ceremony while they're plummeting to the earth. Have you seen it? The marriage vows of an eagle are a lot like that. The marriage vows of the eagle are made at an altitude between ten to fifteen thousand feet by locking talons together, feet to feet, and turning head over heels. This monumental moment in the eagles' life is also enhanced with both birds screaming in joy. Having made these vows, the eagles remain together for life, for richer and poorer, in sickness and in health, until separates them. They truly know what commitment is.

Eagles are one of the only birds that mate for life. Other birds play around; find other partners, but not eagles. Eagles are committed to each other. Even if the female eagle were to die, the male eagle would take the responsibility of raising the baby eagles until they are mature enough to leave home. However, if they are no babies at home, a male eagle will not waste anytime trying to find another mate. They are committed to one partner for their entire life.

This is a perfect picture of a Christian marriage. If part of the animal kingdom is so faithful to their mate, then why shouldn't we be? We are called to be faithful to our mate for life.

Not only is this a picture of faithfulness in Christian marriage, but it is also an invitation to faithfulness in our relationship with the Lord. In Ephesians 5, Paul instructs the people to love their wives with whole-hearted devotion and for the wives to love their husbands back. However, even though uses the imagery of a hus-band and wife, he is actually speaking about Christ and the Church (see Ephesians 5:22-33).

> Husbands, love your wives, just as Christ also loved the church and gave Himself for her, that He might sanctify and cleanse her with the washing of water by the word, that He might present her to Himself a glorious church, not having spot or wrinkle or any such thing, but that she should be holy and without blemish.
>
> Ephesians 5:25-27

The Nest And Habitat

When the pair of eagles have made these vows, they start to build a home together. Eagles will never build a home together without first entering into a marriage covenant. Here is the beau-tiful process where they often fly down to the ground to pick up sticks and flying them as high as ten thousand feet up in the crack of two large rock formations. Here, they have found the perfect spot and the building program starts.

There are not many materials available at that altitude so they have to go all the way down in the valleys to pick up sticks, rocks, or whatever else they can find for the construction of their home. They continue this incredible process of flying up and down until the nest is complete.

Some of the frame of the nest is large sticks – as large as a four-inch diameter and eight feet in length. Building upon it, the sticks would get smaller in diameter until they are ready to put on the final cabinetwork. The limbs have reduced in size now to a one-inch diameter and they continue this until the beautiful home is completed. They do some beautiful decorating of the nest using vines woven together, then leaves that add the soft "homey" affect and then, maybe, some fur to make the home warm and soft enough for the baby eagles that will later be born.

The nest, or what is called an aerie, is made of twigs and sticks built at a point high in a tree or on a cliff edge where they have the greatest visibility. If the eagle chooses a tree, it will usually be a fork in the tree. A cliff is definitely preferred over a tree, but sometimes a tree will suffice if no cliff is around. They try not to build their nest in the top of a tree because it can be violated much easier than on a face of a cliff. They do not build their nests on top of the cliff either, because there it can also be violated. Eagles will try to build their nests in the most inaccessible places in the face of the cliff. That way a predator has to climb up or climb down the cliff to attack the nest. This makes them very insusceptible to attacks from other types of animals.

Their nests are lined with feathers, moss, and leaves so that it is a very comfortable place for them to rest and raise their young. Their nest is added to year after year with the refuse from the previous nests decomposing beneath the newer twigs and sticks that have been added. Their nests average about five feet in diameter and two feet in depth; because they are added to year after year, their nests can become enormous. There have been some nests that measured up to ten feet across, twenty feet deep, and weighing close to two thousand pounds!

Eagles usually live and build their homes near large bodies of water like lakes, rivers, marshes, and seacoasts where there are plenty of fish to eat and many trees and crags to nest in. Eagles are territorial in their nesting – they will live in the same nest, or at least the same area all of their lives. The territory the eagles stay within averages about one to two square miles, much of which is used for hunting. Because of their size, they have few enemies and require larger hunting areas. They will do anything to keep other eagles away from their nesting area.

The Believer's Nest

The Word of God to the believer is as the nest is to the eagle. Just as a nest protects an eagle, the Word of God is our protection, our shield from the enemy of our soul. The written Word gives you a strategic view of the world around you showing you where to fly and not to fly, warning you of dangers out in the big world. When your launching pad is God's eternal Word, you are able to soar like an eagle.

We are to add to our knowledge and understanding of the Word of God day after day, year after year. We are to continually build truth upon the truth God has previously revealed to us. That is God's method of teaching. God will bring revelation after revelation and each measure of revelation is to build on the previous measure of revelation God has already revealed. Isaiah said it this way:

> For precept must be upon precept, precept upon
> precept,
> Line upon line, line upon line,
> Here a little, there a little.
> (Isaiah 28:10)

We are not only to be hearers of the Word, but we must be doers as well. James says we are to "receive with meekness the implanted word" which is able to save our souls (James 1:21). Each time we receive the Word of God with a pure heart, that Word is implanted or engrafted into our souls. It becomes intertwined with who we are – it becomes part of us. As the Word becomes part of us, we begin to do those things in the Word without even being conscious of

> Therefore lay aside all filthiness and overflow of wickedness, and receive with meekness the implanted word, which is able to save your souls.
>
> James 1:21

what we are doing. Beloved, the word is planted in our life in order to produce good and beneficial fruit.

We must be a people that put into practice the things that we hear. We are in an age where information is abundant. If we want to learn about a particular subject, it is only as far away as our fingertips. Books abound about anything we could ever want to learn about. I believe we have more information now that in all previous generations combined. However, we have often confused information with transformation. We have settled with a head knowledge about a subject and equated that with the transformation of the heart.

However, Jesus said that we should be "take heed" with what we hear. He said, "With the same measure that you use, it will be measured to you; and to you who hear, more will be given" (Mark 4:24). It is only as we hear and put into practice the things that we hear, will our lives be changed. Beloved, if all we ever do is go around and get more information, our lives will not be changed. For the Biblical authors, "to hear" meant to fully understand, comprehend, and walk it out in life.

Everything that we do in life must be founded on the Word of the Lord. We want to live a life of such intimacy with the Holy Spirit that He guides us and directs us in every decision that we make. We are not to be like the unwise man who built his house on sand. Rather, Jesus said we are to be like a wise man who built his house on the rock. The storms came and the winds blew, and unlike the unwise man who built on sand, the wise man's house was still standing when it was all said and done (see Matthew 7:24-27). The Word of God is our sure foundation in times of trouble.

When you establish your life on the Rock, on the eternal Word of God, then when the storms of life come, they can't shake your nest. Because your nest has been added to year after year, revelation has been continually added to it, you cannot be shaken in the storms of life. There has been too much of the Word implanted in your heart. Nothing can shake you!

It is vital for us to build our life on the Word of God in the age when everything that can be shaken is going to be shaken. The author of Hebrews says that we must listen carefully to His voice so that "the things which cannot be shaken may remain" (see Hebrews 12:25-29). If we are living our life based upon what He has spoken to us, then when the storms of life come, we will still be standing. Building our life upon the Solid Rock of Jesus is not

> Therefore whoever hears these sayings of Mine, and does them, I will liken him to a wise man who built his house on the rock: and the rain descended, the floods came, and the winds blew and beat on that house; and it did not fall, for it was founded on the rock.
> But everyone who hears these sayings of Mine, and does not do them, will be like a foolish man who built his house on the sand: and the rain descended, the floods came, and the winds blew and beat on that house; and it fell. And great was its fall.
>
> Matthew 7:24-27

optional in this day in age if we want to remain faithful until the end.

Now that we've seen how an eagle finds a mate and builds a home, let us now look at how it controls the air. The eagle is king of the air and seems to use every air current to its advantage. We are going to look at two specific kinds of eagles, namely the Golden and Imperial Eagles, and see how we can draw powerful spiritual implications for our lives.

CHAPTER TEN

The Eagle Is King

Reigning Like A King

WITHOUT QUESTION, THE EAGLE IS THE KING OF THE AIR. THERE IS NO other bird in the entire world that seems to control the air and use it to its advantage as the eagle does. All other birds seem to be moved about with the wind and flap their wings to go from place to place.

The eagle knows how to control the air so that it can get the greatest benefit from the air currents. It doesn't appear to strive through the wind as other birds do. The eagle seems to soar so effortlessly in the midst of every storm that comes its way.

Just as an eagle is king of the air, we're called to be kings and priests in this present life. We're to rule and reign through the authority that Christ has given us – the same authority He had while He was physically present upon the earth. Paul says in Romans 5:17, "For if by the one man's offense death reigned through the one, much more those who receive abundance of grace and of the gift of righteousness will reign in life through the One, Jesus Christ."

Beloved, we're called to reign over every circumstance in life that is not the will of God for us through the power of the Holy

Spirit we are called to know the movings of the Spirit and be obedient to those. When we know from the Word of God or the illumination of the Spirit that something we're going through is not the will of God, we have been given authority to rule over that circumstance. The Amplified Version brings out this verse with a little more clarity when it says:

> For if because of one man's trespass (lapse, offense) death reigned through that one, much more surely will those who receive [God's] overflowing grace (unmerited favor) and the free gift of righteousness [putting them into right standing with Himself] reign as kings in life through the one Man Jesus Christ (the Messiah, the Anointed One). (Romans 5:17, The Amplified Bible)

See that? The Amplified Bible brings out the Greek word a little more when it says we're to "reign as kings in life" through Jesus. We are not to live defeated in the realm of sin and its effects upon our life. We are not ruled by sin, but we are ruled by the power of Christ. We're called to rise above the natural realm with the wings of an eagle and soar high above our circumstances.

Even though the Bald Eagle is the most popular species of eagle in North America, the Bible usually is speaking of a different type of eagle when it makes reference to them. When Scripture refers to the eagle, it is usually referring to the Golden Eagle or the Imperial Eagle. They are a completely different species of eagle than the Bald Eagle; however, their characteristics and attributes are very similar as we learned previously. The names alone of the Golden and Imperial Eagles show many spiritual insights from these magnificent birds. Let's take a look at them.

Golden Eagle

Gold has been a symbol of divinity in history for hundreds of years in different countries and cultures. Gold, throughout history, has frequently represented wealth, value, and kingship. Usually, it was only the royal family that possessed the most amount of gold in any given culture. In fact, most poor people were considered poor because they didn't have any gold – not because they didn't have houses or food. Throughout history gold has been the monetary currency that never depreciates if the economy happens to collapse.

> Gold is a symbol of divinity. He has been used throughout history to represent wealth, value, and kingship. We have a divine nature placed in us after being born of the Spirit.

The name Golden implies divinity to the eagle. It also implies that, as *eagle believers*, we also have a divine nature placed in us after our salvation experience. The divine nature we possess is meant to continually transform our lives on every level over time. It is not a complete and instantaneous change that takes place, though there is an immediate change in a person's life

117

when they are born again. It is as we live by the power of the Holy Spirit that we are changed from one degree of glory to the next degree.

This is Paul's point when he reminds the Corinthians that the Spirit of the Lord brings liberty and freedom to every area of their lives. He says, "Now the Lord is the Spirit; and where the Spirit of the Lord is, there is liberty. But we all, with unveiled face, beholding as in a mirror the glory of the Lord, are being transformed into the same image from glory to glory, just as by the Spirit of the Lord" (2 Corinthians 3:17-18). When we live by the divine nature that was placed in us at the point of salvation, the Holy Spirit is in control of our lives.

Does everyone who is born again have a divine nature? Peter writes to a group of people and tells them that God has given us everything we will ever need to live a life of godliness and fullness. Here is how he greets the people he is writing to in his second letter:

> Grace and peace be multiplied to you in the knowledge of God and of Jesus our Lord, as His divine power has given to us all things that pertain to life and godliness, through the knowledge of Him who called us by glory and virtue, by which have been given to us exceedingly great and precious promises, that through these you may be partakers of the divine nature, having

escaped the corruption that is in the world through lust. (2 Peter 1:2-4)

It is through the promises the Lord has given to us, mainly in His Word is what is being implied here, that we are partakers of the divine nature. We are able to escape the corruption the world teaches by living from our spirit everyday of our lives. We can live *from* Someone greater than ourselves while we are living *for* Him.

This is why Paul said, "Walk in the Spirit, and you shall not fulfill the lust of the flesh. For the flesh lusts against the Spirit, and the Spirit against the flesh; and these are contrary to one another, so that you do not do the things that you wish. But if you are led by the Spirit, you are not under the law" (Galatians 5:16-18). It is only as we live and partake of the divine nature that we are able to overcome our ungodly, fleshly desires.

I love how Eugene Peterson translates the opening statements of Peter in THE MESSAGE. Notice how Peter refers to how Jesus has changed his life as well as the people to whom he is writing to.

I, Simon Peter, am a servant and apostle of Jesus Christ. I write this to you whose experience with God is as life-changing as ours, all due to our God's straight dealing and the intervention of our God and Savior, Jesus Christ. Grace and peace to you many times over as you deepen in your experience with God and Jesus, our Master. Everything that goes into a life of pleasing God has been miraculously given to us by getting to know, personally and intimately, the One who invited us to God. The best invitation we ever received! We were also given absolutely terrific promises to pass on to you – your tickets to participation in the life of God after you turned your back on a world corrupted by lust. (2 Peter 2:1-4, The Message)

Friends, we can participate in the life of God by the promises He has given to us. The divine nature that Peter is talking about is nothing more than walking in the Spirit or living in the God-kind of life.

We have our ultimate model for life contained in the person of Jesus Christ. He lived constantly from the divine nature placed in Him. Even though He was God, He didn't walk the earth as God. Rather, He put aside His divine attributes and walked the earth as a human being under the power of the Holy Spirit. Because we have the Holy Spirit, we can walk in the same way that Jesus did while He was here on the earth.

Jesus lived in perfect righteousness all the days of his life. The author of Hebrews states that "we do not have a High Priest who cannot sympathize with our weaknesses, but was in all points tempted as we are, yet without sin" (Hebrews 4:15). Jesus was tempted by the enemy multiple times throughout His life, yet He overcame every temptation because of the power of the Holy Spirit in His life. Jesus was completely righteous in word and in deed.

Even though Jesus didn't experience sin in His life, Paul tells us that He actually became sin so that we might become righteous. You and I got an F on our report card for life. Jesus, on the other hand, got straight A's. However, Jesus took all of our F's so that we might get straight A's. "For He made Him who knew no sin to be sin for us, that we might become the righteousness of God in Him" (2 Corinthians 5:21).

Friends, if Jesus is our ultimate model and we are able to live life like Him, then why shouldn't we be able to overcome sin in our lives? Why can't we rule and reign as kings in this life through the power of the Holy Spirit? We can because we are partaking of the divine nature that was given to us through the promises of God. The Holy Spirit lives inside each of us and we are able to overcome every obstacle that comes our way.

Imperial Eagle

The name of the second eagle revealed in the Scriptures has very strong implications as well – the Imperial Eagle. The word imperial means having supreme authority and power. The actual word is derived from relating to an empire or emperor. The strength, speed, and majesty of an eagle give it dominion over all the birds and the authority to rule over the heavens. As *eagle believers*, we have also been given the authority to rule the earth with heavenly power. The Apostle John articulates Jesus "has made us kings and priests to His God and Father, to Him be glory and dominion forever and ever..." (Revelation 1:6).

Jesus gave us, what has been called throughout the history of the church, the Great Com-mission. This only came after He said that *all* authority was His. It is only after He describes the realm of His authority that He passes on the Great Commission to His disciples. Jesus is here explaining to *eagle believers* that He has given us authority, and it is only because of this authority that we are able to go and make disciples of all nations. To truly disciple nations, we need to get the mindset of an eagle and learn how to soar in the high places with God. If we don't know how to soar in our full potential, then how can we teach others to soar?

> All authority has been given to Me in heaven and on earth. Go therefore and make disciples of all the nations, baptizing them in the name of the Father and of the Son and of the Holy Spirit, teaching them to observe all things that I have commanded you; and lo, I am with you always, even to the end of the age. Amen.
>
> Matthew 28:18-21

The eagle is a bird of the air created to live in the heavens. It is to have a bird's eye view of all that is below it. God has a heavenly calling for every one of us as believers; a calling that summons us closer to God and further away from the world; a calling that would give us an overview of our situation or direction in the oncoming storm so that we might choose our course. God has raised you and me up to sit in heavenly places with Christ (see Ephesians 2:5-6). He has called us to be heavenly creatures, and to be the head and not the tail, to be above only and not be beneath, to know only victory and not defeat. We must begin to see ourselves as "more than conquerors through Him who loved us" in everything we go through (Romans 8:37). We must see ourselves as eagles – majestic, strong, and free.

"They shall mount up with wings like eagles" (Isaiah 40:31).

What makes an eagle to be able to soar so high in the air? Does it have a secret to soaring on the air thermals? In the next chapter, we're going to look at how eagles are meant to soar and every eagle has the potential in them to soar, whether they recognize it or not.

CHAPTER ELEVEN

The Eagles Flying Secrets

Eagles Are Meant To Soar

EAGLES ARE ABLE TO FLY LIKE ALL OTHER BIRDS. THEY CAN FLAP their wings and go from one place to another with the effort of continual flapping and an output of continual energy. However, that is not what they do best. Eagles have a secret to flying that almost no other bird understands. While all the other types of birds are out flapping their way from place to place, the eagle uses the air currents to soar effortlessly from one place to the next.

Eagles are meant to soar high in the sky, high above any other type of bird that was created. In fact, an eagle lives to soar – part of what makes an eagle an eagle is its ability to soar above the storms of life. That is when an eagle is most alive; when they are soaring high above everything in this world and seeing things from a higher perspective.

When an eagle leaves its nest, it literally jumps into the air, and with one flap of its wings, it is air bound. An eagle seems to take off and soar with ease. It will catch the air currents and can ride them for hours and hours at a time without ever flapping its wings once. The flapping of their wings is only preparatory to get them to the good air currents so they are able to soar high above all else. The eagle has an innate ability to sense the motion of the wind currents.

Most birds will run for cover and not be out flying when a storm comes. Not so with eagles! They love storms! They will perch on a branch and wait for hours for an approaching storm because the storm brings more air currents so the eagle is able to soar higher and fly faster. These air currents force the eagle to soar higher than what it can do on a normal day without the storms and high winds. Some eagles have been known to soar over 10,000 feet high!

Ornithologists, or those who study birds scientifically, "assure us that the eagle...can fly more swiftly against a wind than in a gentle breeze. It may be that this is because they are stimulated to exert the muscular strength of their pinions. But however this may be, it is a fact that the fires of a steamship burn much more fiercely under the boilers when the vessel is going against a headwind."[vii] According to those who know about birds, eagles were made to soar in the storms.

> An eagle experiences more life and vitality when it is soaring above the storms of life. An eagle is meant to soar - it lives to soar.

[vii] Tan, P. L. (1996, c1979). *Encyclopedia of 7700 Illustrations: [A Treasury of Illustrations, Anecdotes, Facts and Quotations for Pastors, Teachers and Christian Workers]*. Garland TX: Bible Communications.

There is an incident recorded when the late Steve McQueen flew a glider in the Rocky Mountains. He hit an air thermal (also known as an updraft) and he decided to ride it as far as it would take him. He got extremely high for a glider, somewhere between an estimated fourteen and fifteen thousand feet. He looked out the window of his glider and was amazed at what he saw. Was it beautiful territory from a bird's eye view? Was it beautiful mountain peaks that were capped with snow? I'm sure he was amazed by these sights. However, he mentions only one thing that he saw. He said,

> "You'll never guess. I saw eagles! They had the ability to lock their wings. It looked like they were asleep; they were just riding the wind so effortlessly."[viii]

He says these eagles looked like they were asleep because of the graceful glide on the currents of the wind! What an amazing sight this must have been!

The Eaglets' Potential

Even though the eagle is king of the air, it has to know it is king before it has the authority to rule the air. Baby eagles have

---

[viii] Fullam, Terry, *Life On Wings*. This quote was taken from a sermon by Pastor Bob Stone entitled *With Eagles Wings: How Eagles Reflect Our Spiritual Journey*. It was accessed off of http://www.eagleflight.org/cyberSermons/growing_church/eagles_wings.html on September 5, 2006.

all the potential to be king of the air. There is only one problem with it: they have to know how to fly and use the air currents to their advantage. Just because they were created for something so great doesn't necessarily mean they are going to fulfill it in their lives.

Hosea faced much of the same problem in his day. God had called the Israelites to be so much more than what they had become. Once again, Israel was backslidden; there wasn't any truth, mercy, or intimacy with God in the whole land. Then the Lord spoke through Hosea that He was rejecting them from being priests because they had rejected knowledge. God said, "My people are destroyed for lack of knowledge. Because you have rejected knowledge, I also will reject you from being priest for Me" (Hosea 4:6).

Do you see the principle contained here? Because they didn't take time to seek God to find out who they were to be and do, they were destroyed because of their lack of knowledge. They were called for so much more than what they were actually fulfilling in their lives. God rejected them from their priestly office – who they were called to be and what they were called to do - because they didn't take time to find out what their identity was. If we don't ever take time to figure out who we are in Christ, or, better yet, who Christ is in us, then we will never fulfill our God-given role in life. We can only fulfill all our potential when we know our identity in Christ.

Friends, we have to learn how to fly and to soar on wings like eagles. We are created for so much more than what we truly know or even realize in our present existence. We are created to soar high above the storms of life and be the exceeding conqueror through Jesus Christ that Paul mentions (see Romans 8:37). We are created to see every situation in our life from His perspective. When we see from God's perspective, things look a lot clearer.

Have you ever flown in an airplane before? Sometimes it is so cloudy you cannot see a thing when you are on the ground driving to the airport. Then you get in the plane and you begin to fly and it is still cloudy. Then you get to a certain height, then all of the sudden, you break through the clouds and it

> The eaglet has all of the potential to be king of the air. However, for the eaglet to rule the air, it will have to know how to use the air currents to its advantage.

is as clear and calm as ever. When it is clear, you can see for hundreds of miles out the window of the airplane. You can look out and see everything according to the big picture, or, the way God sees it. You can see how lakes relate to mountains; how houses and streets look so close to each other and so small. We don't know about all the traffic jams that are taking place, the stop lights, or the road construction delays that we passed through on our way to the airport because we are seeing things from a different perspective.

That is exactly how God wants us to see and look at our situations. He wants us to put our struggles of today into His ultimate purpose and look at everything in our lives from His perspective. We have to break through the clouds of our circumstances and see things from the ultimate perspective of God. Our situations will look much clearer from the way He sees them.

Stirring The Nest

When a baby eagle is born, it finds its home is very soft and secure; a cozy nest high up in a secure place and mama and papa are very good parents. They make the nest as comfortable as possible for the little one. There, the eagle happily grows until it reaches eighty percent of its full body size and weight at about three months of age. Momma and daddy are so proud of the eaglet while the it is safely tucked into the nest all the while growing bigger and bigger. The daddy goes and finds toys on the ground and brings it to the nest just for his eagle babies. Isn't that the way we daddies are? We go out and buy toys for the little ones so they can play and have a fun time.

Everything seems to be going fine for the eaglet. It is enjoying life with its toys in the comfort of the nest. To be honest, a lot of us in church are very comfortable with our toys and we like to sit comfortably in our nest not wanting to get out of our comfort zone. It is about the time that the eaglet gets comfortable that one day, mama and papa start behaving very strangely. They are no longer comforting the eaglet in the same ways as before. It is time for the eaglet to learn to soar – to not be so dependent on its parents.

Moses, speaking for the Lord, tells us how the young eagles get their introduction to the practice of soaring in the heavens. Let the *eagle saints* hear this carefully. It says the mother eagle "stirs up its nest, Hovers over its young, Spreading out its wings, taking them up, carrying them on its wings" (Deuteronomy 32:11). The time has come for the young eagle to leave the comfort of her nest and launch out on its own. Eugene Peterson, in THE MESSAGE translation of the Bible, describes the scene this way:

> He found him [referring to Israel] out in the
>   wilderness, in an empty, windswept wasteland.
> He threw his arms around him, lavished atten-
>   tion on him, guarding him as the apple of his
>   eye.
> He was like an eagle hovering over its nest,
>   overshadowing its young,
> Then spreading its wings, lifting them into the
>   air, teaching them to fly.
> God alone led him;
>   there was not a foreign god in sight.
> God lifted him onto the hilltops,
>   so he could feast on the crops in the fields.
> He fed him honey from the rock,
>   oil from granite crags,

Curds of cattle and the milk of sheep,

the choice cuts of lambs and goats,

Fine Bashan rams, high-quality wheat,

and the blood of grapes: you drank good wine!

(Deuteronomy 32:10-14, THE MESSAGE)

The time has come for the eaglet to leave the nest and move out on its own. The eaglet is now old enough to begin to live life on its own. Looking down from the dizzying heights of the mountain peak, it is not ready to begin such a dangerous endeavor. It has not passed this way before and is very reluctant to begin to go this way. We often get so uncomfortable with things we haven't experienced before. At the very core of our nature, we don't like change. However, Jesus came for that very purpose – to change our inner man. He came to transform our heart.

Therefore, the mother eagle begins making things uncomfortable for the eaglet in the nest. First, she doesn't bring any goodies to eat any longer. Up until this time, mama and papa would bring the eaglet food day after day, sometimes multiple times a day. Now papa, and especially mama, are acting more strange and peculiar than ever before. I am sure the eaglets think that maybe mama eagle has PMS because of the intense change in her mood!

Not only do they stop bringing any food; but they start grabbing hunks of the comfortable nest and dropping it over the side. Mama is making it uncomfortable for her babies to continue life as normal in the nest. The nest has been so safe, so comfortable, and the eaglets are satisfied to remain there. Mama eagle continues to tear up the nest, breaking the twigs, ripping the comfortable lining out, until the jagged ends of the sticks are poking out. In other words, she begins to make life very miserable for her babies in the place that once had seemed so nice and comfortable.

Do we have anybody in Church experiencing that in this present season of their lives? It seems like God is taking away some of our comfort zone – it is getting very hard to sit comfortably in our pews or chairs on Sunday morning. God is starting to stir up something in our hearts and lives. We don't know what it is because we have never felt it before. This stirring up is something completely foreign to us. What seemed so comfortable before is now becoming very uncomfortable to us. Why does God do this to us? Because we'll never soar as long as our nest is lined with feathers, leaves, and skins of rabbits and other mammals. The nest is too comfortable to leave. God does this because He knows that we are created for so much more in our lives – He realizes our full potential in Him. We are not meant to do Church as normal. We are meant to be the Church in a supernatural way.

Created To Soar

You are an *eagle believer*. An *eagle believer* is born to soar, not to play around with baby toys in a comfortable nest enjoying a cozy atmosphere for their whole life. That is fine for a season in our life when we are first born of the Spirit. Now, beloved, it is time to soar! It is time to spread out our wings like an eagle and learn to soar in the midst of storms. It is time to fly high like an eagle! It is time to learn to hunt like an eagle; to face storms and serpents like an eagle; to be able to face our enemy and to provide fresh food for our families and for ourselves. It is time for the eaglets to grow up and be mature!

Mama and papa pay no attention as the eaglets begin to cry

> An eagle believer is born to soar. They are not called to sit around in the comfortable nest of life. They are called to get out of the nest and learn to soar through the storms of life.

because of their being uncomfortable. She takes her huge talons, picks up, and places the baby on the edge of the nest. The eaglet is very upset by this as it looks over the edge and is completely scared to death. It cries out to mama and papa wondering why they are doing this to it. "Why are you doing this to me, papa and mama?" Doesn't that sound very familiar? Jesus said something very similar while He hung on the cross, "My God, My God, why have You forsaken Me?" (Matthew 27:46). "Why are you allowing these things to happen to me? Why are things so uncomfortable in my work situation, at my church, in my finances, in my home?"

Suddenly, without warning, mama eagle pushes the baby over the edge. This begins a free-fall and the baby eagle is completely helpless. It appears the eaglet is doomed to be smashed on the rocks below. It is bewildered at why mama would do this to it.

Before mama pushes the eaglet over, the male eagle will fly overhead circling to watch everything that is taking place. He is always ready to sweep underneath to catch the eaglet before it hits the ground. This is exactly what our Father does when we are learning to soar. He is flying high above us watching everything that takes place in our lives. How comforting it must be to know that our Father is watching over us throughout every part of our lives.

The reason for all of the circumstances surrounding our lives is that God is giving us an invitation to soar. Many of us, however, have not yet responded to the invitation to soar on eagles' wings. Because of this, God is taking us to the edge of our nest, so that we can peer over and see what we were created for, what our destiny is, and what our purpose in this life is. You are not created to only make it to heaven. God has given you purpose and a destiny to advance His kingdom here on earth as it is in heaven.

Is your nest being stirred these days? Did you ever think it might be your heavenly Father trying to teach you how to soar? Did it ever cross your mind that God is about to do something major in your life and He is trying to get you to see things from His perspective. Again, remember Deuteronomy 32:11-12?

As an eagle stirs up its nest,

Hovers over its young,

Spreading out its wings, taking them up,

Carrying them on its wings,

So the LORD alone led him,

And there was no foreign god with him.

It was the Lord who led the Israelites out of Egypt. The Israelites couldn't see what they were created for because they were in such tremendous bondage. The Lord took them to the edge of the nest and pushed them over the side of it so they could step into their full potential – to worship the Lord in the wilderness and eventually to get to the Promised Land.

You and I were born to soar like an eagle! Don't be afraid to look over the nest, God is pushing you into your destiny! Spread your wings wide, catch the air currents, and begin to soar like an eagle!

Even though we are created to soar, we must have the strength to be able to soar. In the next chapter, we will look at the *eagle believer's* source of strength.

CHAPTER TWELVE

The Eagles Source Of Strength

You Are What You Eat

IN OUR PRESENT STUDY OF THE EAGLE, IT IS IMPORTANT TO UNDER-
stand the source of strength of an eagle. Have you ever heard
the saying, "you are what you eat"? This, of course, is inferring
that one's diet affects one's strength and health. The same is
true when we're talking about eagles. Eagles will try to eat only
fresh food on a daily basis. Experts estimate that about ninety
percent of an eagles' diet is fresh fish. They have been known to
eat many other types of small mammals, but it seems they prefer
fish over everything else. That is why, in North America, the majority of Bald Eagles are found in the state of Alaska, where they
are constantly around fresh water to catch fish.

The main difference in eagles and others in the bird family is
that eagles pick their diet; they usually are not left to be scaven-
gers or to eat what has already been killed. Other birds are willing to eat worms, berries, insects, and carcasses of highway
tragedies because that is what they are used to and it is all they
can sometimes get. This is not true of eagles. Eagles will only

eat carrion if they are extremely hungry and cannot find fresh food anywhere else.

Eagles are birds that pick their diet. They will eat fish today, squirrel tomorrow, and maybe some rabbit the next day. They can eat anything their heart desires, granted it is fresh and it is what they are in the mood for. The eagle does not eat what it finds; it finds what it wants to eat.

Eagles sit at the top of the food chain. This means they are more susceptible to toxins and poisons because the toxins are able to go through each animal or plant that has been eaten. Toxins are passed from animal to animal, until they end up in the eagle. Because an eagle is toward the top of the food chain attributes to one of the reasons the Bald Eagle was almost extinct and on the endangered species list for a number of years.

> Eagles choose what they want to eat. We, in the same way, should be careful and choose wisely what we feast upon.

God is calling us to do the same thing; to know what He is calling us to be and go after that. We are not to settle for the way the world is going through life and eating from the world's buffet because the pollution is going to affect our spiritual life. We are not to be conformed to the world's present standards, but we're to be transformed by the way we think. It is only as we change the way we think that we'll know what God's perfect will is for our lives.

Listen to what Paul tells the Romans:

> I beseech you therefore, brethren, by the mercies of God, that you present your bodies a living sacrifice, holy, acceptable to God, which is your reasonable service. And do not be conformed to this world, but be transformed by the renewing of your mind, that you may prove what is that good and acceptable and perfect will of God. (Romans 12:1-2)

Too many of us have been eating from what we hear on television or the negative reports society is feeding us through the news. We need to get rid of all the food that is polluting us and stopping us from flying and fulfilling our full potential in Him. Instead of soaring, we settle in the chicken yard, all the while knowing that there is a big eagle in each one of us waiting to find the freedom to be able to soar again.

> We are to be transformed by the renewing of our mind. This will only come when our main diet is the Word of God.

There is a battle going on for the hearts and minds of men and women throughout the world. When Paul was writing to the Corinthians, He was telling them that they are to demolish every "stronghold" that was in their mind. The enemy tries to set up these strongholds in our mind so that it affects the truth that enters our heart.

Paul defines what a stronghold is when he says that they are "arguments and every high thing that exalts itself against the knowledge of God" (2 Corinthians 10:5). Even though the enemy is trying to block or distort the truth that we perceive with our minds and finally enters our hearts, God says that we must bring "every thought into captivity to the obedience of Christ" (see 2 Corinthians 10:1-6). Jesus came to bring us truth which is able to set us free (see John 8:32).

Choose Your Diet

The eagle does not rely on what it finds; it finds what it wants, what it was created to do. The eagle chooses its diet for the day and then goes to find it. Once finding its meal, it will dive down to lay hold of it, crushing the life from it with its strong talons. The eagle will then ascend to its nest and pull the prey apart while it is still warm and fresh.

We need to remember a poor spiritual diet is going to produce poor spiritual health in our lives. Our spiritual tolerance of today's battles of life will be totally affected by what we eat. If the only time we are fed is in our Sunday morning services, then we are not going to be very strong in our walk with the Lord. If that is the only time we eat from the Lord's table, then we are eating food that has already been chewed and spit back out. It was someone else's revelation.

It is necessary for us to be able to have time alone with God, reading the Bible and soaking in His presence. It is important for us as *eagle believers* to get around other *eagle believers* who think and talk like eagles and who want to soar in the higher places than what they have previously experienced. This is so we are able to experience fellowship and enjoy the revelation of being on the top of a Rock – Jesus Christ – experiencing the Most High through worship, fellowship, intimacy, soaking, and warfare.

Our discernment for our appetite must be very clear. Like the eagle, we must choose our spiritual diet and eat only that. Jesus said that we are to be *in* the world, but not *of* the world (see John 17). Our spirit man has an incredible appetite for spiritual nourishment. We need to hunt and peck after what our spirit desires so that we are able to get ahold of the spiritual nutrition we need to be able to soar in the high places. Like the eagle, we desire living food and refuse to go after the world's dead food. Part of the living food we find is in the Word of God. The author of Hebrews states,

> For the word of God is living and powerful, and sharper than any two-edged sword, piercing even to the division of soul and spirit, and of joints and marrow, and is a discerner of the thoughts and intents of the heart. And there is no creature hidden from His sight, but all things are

> naked and open to the eyes of Him to whom we
> must give account. (Hebrews 4:12-13)

The Bible says that the Word is alive and full of power. However, Jesus states that our traditions can make His Word powerless in our lives and the lives of others. If we are mixing His Word with our human-made traditions, then we are taking the effect the Word will have on our life and others lives, and making it completely powerless (see Matthew 15:6). Therefore, the Word of God should be the main course of every *eagle saint* in our daily lives. We should be feasting on the Word of God everyday. I'm not saying that we have to do this for hours a day and we're not allowed to watch TV or read the newspaper. That is not very practical.

Nevertheless, we must make it a point everyday to feast on the Word of God. You can read it in the morning, afternoon or night – whatever is the best time for you. We are all individuals and God speaks to each of us in different ways. Ask yourself this question: "What do I primarily feast on everyday?" How you answer that question will determine where your priorities are in your life? Ask again, "Where do I want to spend the majority of my time feasting?" We must close the gap between where we are at presently and where we want to be in the future.

Feasting on the Word must be something we do for ourselves. We're not to primarily listen to others talk about their experiences with the Lord and what God has been speaking to them. We cannot live off of the fresh revelation and experiences of others. Sure, it is wonderful to hear what God is speaking to others. But, if that is all we ever eat, then we are going to be spiritually weak people.

An eagle can watch another eagle eat all the food in the world. The eagle can even listen to the other eagle talk about how good the meal was. However, if the eagle never eats any-thing itself, it will die of starvation. In the same way, if we only hear the Word being preached with-out ever partaking of it ourselves, we will die spiritually. Don't get me wrong here. I love hearing preachers and even preaching myself. It is something God has instituted in the Church so that we can be taught, learn, and grow in the ways of Christ. But I must have my own meals and my own spiritual diet in order to survive with the fullest possible life Jesus has destined for me.

> If the eagle never eats anything itself, it will die of starvation. In the same way, if we only hear the Word being preached without ever partaking of it our-selves, we will die spiritually.

Paul writes a very powerful word to the Galatian believers. He tells them if they walk in the Spirit, they will not want to fulfill the desires of their flesh (see Galatians 5). Our pursuit must be one of pursuing and walking in intimacy with the Spirit of God. As we follow Him with all of our hearts, then we will not fulfill our earthly desires – what our flesh wants to do. We won't want to sin and live in the ways of the world because of the nature of God that we possess in our lives. In the same way, while we are

143

able to fly and soar in high places we will not be satisfied with being down on earth in the chicken yard continually flapping with clipped wings. We are not going to be able to soar in the high places with clipped wings.

If the only meal we ever eat is what someone else has told us about, or if we are eating from the table of the world, then we look more like a vulture than an eagle. The vulture builds its nest in dead trees or on the ground. A vultures head and neck are featherless and hairless so that it can more readily stick its head into corrupted carcasses for its meals. The diet of the vulture is the diet of leftovers. After circling over its meat for hours to make sure it is dead, the vulture descends, usually accompanied by others who do not want the solitary lifestyle of the eagle. There is nothing finicky, meticulous, or even tasteful about the vulture's diet. The vulture will eat until it becomes intoxicated with blood by overeating. Then it is unable to fly and often becomes prey itself.

We see this with many believers who are going after the things the world has to offer, even the leftovers from the world. They are not able to experience soaring in the high places and to be able to experience the sun, the wind, the storms, and the Most High, which are all part of the *eagle saints* lifestyle.

The vulture is an easy target for its enemies so it becomes the prey. Our calling is to be an eagle but many believers settle to be a vulture. The spiritual vulture would gorge itself so much on many activities like fellowship and entertainment that it would not be able to fly and endure the hardships of life, and so becomes the prey of its enemy. While it is feasting on the dead carcass of some animal, another animal will come and eat the vulture because it has become so fat with its present meal.

The *eagle saints* will seek out live prey and draw their strength from the the voice of their Father. An *eagle believer* will seek food and solitude, being alone with the One that made him, on the high places and not become involved in the corruption of gossip, idleness, negativism, bitterness, and lack of forgiveness.

The *eagle saint* is the strongest and most beautiful of all Christians because he has found a source of health and strength. The Bible says,

> My son, give attention to my words;
> Incline your ear to my sayings.
> Do not let them depart from your eyes;
> Keep them in the midst of your heart;
> For they are life to those who find them,
> And health to all their flesh.
> (Proverbs 4:20-22)

CHAPTER THIRTEEN

The Eagles Secret To Life

DID YOU KNOW THAT AN EAGLE HAS A SECRET TO LIFE? DO YOU know what that secret is? An eagle's secret to life is found in the waiting process that it endures to gain new strength. After it has learned the secret of quietness and expectant waiting, then it gains new life and vitality.

Let us read the Isaiah passage again in a different translation of the Bible:

> Why, O Jacob, do you say, and declare, O Israel,
> My way and my lot are hidden from the Lord, and
> my right is passed over without regard from my
> God?
> Have you not known? Have you not heard? The
> everlasting God, the Lord, the Creator of the ends
> of the earth, does not faint or grow weary; there is
> no searching of His understanding.
> He gives power to the faint and weary, and to him
> who has no might He increases strength [causing
> it to multiply and making it to abound]. [2 Cor
> 12:9.]

Even youths shall faint and be weary, and [se-
lected] young men shall feebly stumble and fall
exhausted;

But those who wait for the Lord [who expect, look
for, and hope in Him] shall change and renew
their strength and power; they shall lift their wings
and mount up [close to God] as eagles [mount up
to the sun]; they shall run and not be weary, they
shall walk and not faint or become tired. [Heb
12:1-3.]

(Isaiah 40:27-31, The Amplified Bible)

The secret to the life of the eagle is mounting up close to the
sun and soaring in that place. We are to continually wait on the
Lord so that we get fresh strength. Beloved, this new set of
feathers isn't going to come by sitting back and doing nothing
with your life. You are to wait for the Lord; you are to expect, look
for, and hope in the Lord. This is to be done with eager expectation until He shows up and does something powerful in your life.

The secret of success in your life is found in waiting on the
Lord with eager expectation. You may look successful in your life
outwardly – you may preach at many conferences and travel all
over the world with the Gospel - like I was. However, your success isn't found it that. You can only have true and lasting success in your life as you wait on the Lord. "Well, Leif. I'm too busy
to pray. I have too much to do today." Listen to me: You are too
busy *not* to pray. Your life and vitality depends on you waiting on

God everyday of your life. Continue to wait on Him with prayer, fasting, Bible study, soaking, and warfare. As you do this, you will experience a fresh set of feathers – you will experience fresh vitality.

You are created to "mount up [close to God] as eagles" and to run and not be weary and walk but not faint. Don't settle with being a chicken in the chicken coup for the rest of your life. You are created to soar! There is something within each of us that knows we were created for something greater than what we are presently experiencing.

Here is a story that I heard in closing that I want to relate to you about an eagle that never found out it was an eagle. It is similar to the story I told you in the beginning of this book, but it has a

"You cannot fly like an eagle with the wings of a wren." – Henry Hudson (An English Sea Explorer and Navigator in the Early Seventeenth Century).

completely different outcome. The eagle in the beginning found out it was an eagle and learned to soar. However, this eagle never finds out its full potential. Which one do you want to be?

There is an old fable, which relates how a man found an egg of an eagle and placed it in a nest of a chicken in the barnyard. The time came for the eagle to hatch, and it was constantly surrounded by chickens. All of its life, the eagle did what he saw the chickens do, thinking that he was a chicken because that is how he grew up.

He scratched the earth for worms and insects. He clucked and cackled like the rest of the chickens. And, like all the other chickens, he would violently flap its wings and only get a few feet in the air because they were continually clipped. Years passed as the eagle continually lived like this and it grew very old.

One day, the eagle looked up from the barnyard that he was living in, into the magnificent sky above. The eagle saw something that it had never seen before. He saw a huge magnificent bird in the cloudless sky. This bird glided so gracefully among the powerful wind currents, without a beat of its strong wings. The old eagle continued to stare in total amazement. "Who's that?" he asked. "That's the eagle, the king of the birds," said his neighbor. "He belongs to the sky. We belong to the earth – we're chickens."

The old eagle lived and died a chicken, for that is what he thought he was. What you surround yourself with is what you become. Solomon said, "For as [a man] thinks in his heart, so is he" (Proverbs 23:7, Brackets mine). You are not called to live in the chicken yard any longer with chickens. You are created for soaring like an eagle! Don't let anything hold you back from your true potential and destiny!

APPENDIX A

List Of Eagle Scriptures

LISTED BELOW IS A COMPREHENSIVE LIST OF SCRIPTURES NAMING, or relating to eagles throughout the entire Bible. This is provided for your own further study. There are many more things that God has to reveal about *eagle believers* in these last days. Ask the Holy Spirit to illuminate more truth and revelation to you as you study these passages.

There are over thirty-two references to an eagle in the Bible, though there are only thirty Scriptures listed below. In some of the passages below, the eagle is mentioned more than once, resulting in over thirty-two references. It would be helpful to read them in their larger contexts to gain a richer understanding of what the Biblical authors were trying to convey in using the imagery of an eagle.

All of the passages listed below are taken from the New King James Version of the Bible. Some translations might translate the word "eagle" as something else. It will be helpful to check alternate translations if you are having trouble understanding any one of the passages listed below.

1. Exodus 19:1-6

2. Leviticus 11:13

3. Deuteronomy 14:12

4. Deuteronomy 28:49

5. Deuteronomy 32:10-14

6. 2 Samuel 1:23

7. Job 9:25-31

8. Job 39:27-30

9. Psalm 103:1-5

10. Proverbs 23:4-5

11. Proverbs 30:17

12. Proverbs 30:18-19

13. Isaiah 40:27-31

14. Jeremiah 4:13

15. Jeremiah 48:40

16. Jeremiah 49:16, 22

17. Lamentations 4:19

18. Ezekiel 1:10-14

19. Ezekiel 10:14

20. Ezekiel 17:1-10

21. Daniel 7:4

22. Hosea 8:1

23. Obadiah 2-4

24. Micah 1:16

25. Habakkuk 1:8

26. Matthew 24:28

27. Luke 17:37

28. Revelation 4:7-11

29. Revelation 8:12-13

30. Revelation 12:13-14

Soaring As Eagles

Leif Hetland

Like no other bird, eagles hold a special place in the heart of God. The king of the air can be found thirty-two times in scripture – more than any other bird. One of the eagle's greatest gifts is the ability to soar. God is calling a generation of eagle saints that will soar in the heavenlies.

The unique design of eagles gives them many advantages. The eagle, more than any other bird, portrays God – His strength, beauty, solemnity, majesty, fearlessness, and freedom. As we look at the nature of the eagle we will see and appreciate God and come to understand ourselves and how to live as heavenly creatures, to have an overview of all that is below. The eagle Christian is a conqueror and he rules over his domain.

Stop struggling – Start **SOARING!**

The Molting Eagle
Leif Hetland

Christian, are you tired? Discouraged? Overwhelmed? Ready to throw in the towel?

Maybe you are in the middle of a molting season. When you are in the valley of despair and desperation, you will feel at times you are never going to soar again. Can you picture yourself like the molting eagle, eyes dry, losing feathers, talons brittle, no appetite, lonely, oppressed, and no longer catching the winds and soaring above the clouds?

In this teaching, Leif is brutally honest about his molting season and how the example of the eagle's renewal through the molting process helped him to soar again. There is an identity crisis in the body of Christ. Through molting, we will mount up with eagles' wings to soar above the storm clouds in the heavenly realms. Only then will we see the **invisible** and do the **impossible**.

Swift As An Eagle
Leif Hetland

...for they will surely sprout wings and fly off to the sky like an eagle.
Proverbs 23:5

God is up to something - He is gathering His army of Eagle Believers who will rule and reign. There is a shaking going on and everything will be shaken that can be shaken. The one thing that cannot be shaken is the Kingdom of Heaven.

The eagle spends an hour a day cleaning and preparing its feathers before it begins its flight. We must spend time preparing for God's agenda for our future. At such a time as this we need to be Christian Eagles responding swiftly to God's call.

This is a time of opportunity and God wants you involved!

ABOUT THE AUTHOR

L e i f   H e t l a n d
President & Founder of Global Mission Awareness

Leif Hetland established Global Mission Awareness
to reach the unloved, the unreached, and the untold with the
Love of God. He has ministered for 22 years
in 65 countries around the world.

Leif speaks at numerous conferences, churches, crusades, busi-
nesses, and schools in the United States and abroad.
Soaring as Eagles Conferences are an urgent call of God
to prepare Eagle Saints for Supernatural Living.

For more information about Leif Hetland, Global Mission
Awareness, or Soaring as Eagles Conferences,
contact GMA at www.GlobalMissionAwareness.org
or the GMA Office at (256) 768-2585